"Discovering" Risk

ERUPTIONS
New Thinking across the Disciplines

Erica McWilliam
General Editor

Vol. 18

PETER LANG
New York • Washington, D.C./Baltimore • Bern
Frankfurt am Main • Berlin • Brussels • Vienna • Oxford

Judith Bessant, Richard Hil
& Rob Watts

"Discovering" Risk

Social Research and Policy Making

PETER LANG
New York • Washington, D.C./Baltimore • Bern
Frankfurt am Main • Berlin • Brussels • Vienna • Oxford

Library of Congress Cataloging-in-Publication Data
Bessant, Judith.
"Discovering" risk: social research and policy making /
Judith Bessant, Richard Hil, Rob Watts.
p. cm. — (Eruptions; vol. 18)
Includes bibliographical references and index.
1. Risk—Sociological aspects. 2. Social policy. 3. Social problems.
4. Youth with social disabilities—Government policy. 5. Problem youth—
Government policy. I. Hil, Richard. II. Watts, Rob.
III. Title. IV. Eruptions; v. 18.
HM1101 .B47   302'.12—dc21   2002030136
ISBN 0-8204-5813-9
ISSN 1091-8590

Die Deutsche Bibliothek-CIP-Einheitsaufnahme
Bessant, Judith:
"Discovering" risk: social research and policy making /
Judith Bessant; Richard Hil; Rob Watts.
–New York; Washington, D.C./Baltimore; Bern;
Frankfurt am Main; Berlin; Brussels; Vienna; Oxford: Lang.
(Eruptions; Vol. 18)
ISBN 0-8204-5813-9

Cover design by Joni Holst

© 2003 Peter Lang Publishing, Inc., New York
275 Seventh Avenue, 28th Floor, New York, NY 10001
www.peterlangusa.com

All rights reserved.
Reprint or reproduction, even partially, in all forms such as microfilm,
xerography, microfiche, microcard, and offset strictly prohibited.

Table of Contents

Acknowledgments vii

Introduction 1

Chapter One
The Discovery of Risk and the Governmental Project 7

Chapter Two
At Risk of Unemployment 29

Chapter Three
Risk and Homelessness: An Empirical Problem? 53

Chapter Four
Crime and the Science of Risk 71

Chapter Five
Risk and Crime Control: The British Experience 97

Chapter Six
Governance of Social Problems and Problem Populations 115

Conclusion 129

Bibliography 131

Index 145

Acknowledgments

We would especially like to thank Sharon Andrews and Zennie McLoughlin for their support in getting the text ready for publication. There are many other people without whom this book could not have been written including our students upon whom we relied to test some of the ideas and formulations found in this book. We also acknowledge the support of colleagues and friends who over the years have argued with us and offered valuable feedback on our analysis of risk-based research, policy, and thinking.

Although Australian universities are currently not ideal places for the nurturing of research, we are appreciative of the opportunities that are offered to support scholarship and research. In that regard we thank the Australian Catholic University in Melbourne for providing Judith Bessant with a semester's sabbatical, and the School of Social Science and Planning at the Royal Melbourne Institute of Technology University, which provided Rob Watts with six months of research leave in 2001. The University of Southern Cross likewise gave invaluable support to Richard Hil when he much needed it.

Introduction

In the 1980s, and extending into the first decade of the twenty-first century, two words have become, if not obligatory, then certainly widely used parts of the social science vocabulary. One word—"globalisation"—is used in almost magical fashion so that merely invoking it renders any social or economic problem immediately explicable and obviates the need for any clarification. The other word—"risk"—is also used to conjure up the idea that our era seems to throw up all kinds of novel problems for individuals.

Australia, in common with many other countries, is going through a painful process of restructuring. Much of the restructuring has been conveniently explained in terms of "globalisation."[1] For example one politician-commentator, Mark Latham (1998), claims globalisation has re-fashioned the social, political, and economic landscape. "Globalisation," he says (1998), has eroded the traditional barriers and policy practices of the nation-state, and politicians everywhere are "struggling to establish the new tools of national economic sovereignty."[2] Latham"s account, like so much of this analysis, is determinist.[3] Bob Catley epitomises this when he writes, "I came to the conclusion that [these] kinds of structural changes...were inevitable" (1996: ix). The determinist logic of his (1996: 4) argument is simple:

> Globalisation looms large over the future prospects of social democracy. Economic and social restructuring, not surprisingly, has produced elements of political restructuring.

He reiterates the point:

> The restructuring of the world economic order is an event rare in history, especially given the scale of globalisation in recent decades. Economic restructuring inevitably gives rise to new social and political tensions (1996: 9).

While many politicians conveniently blame an irresistible force deemed to be out of their control, a case can be made that much of the restructuring was a political process driven by governments and policy communities who chose to pursue these kinds of policies (Watts 2000). Governments (not globalisation) reduced taxation and cut public expenditures and infrastructure investment as they privatised, downsized, and outsourced their activities. Globalisation has been linked to talk about risk and the increasing evidence of social polarisation.

Risk talk works differently. Although concern about globalisation is far from being an exclusive preoccupation, a considerable part of the anxiety about it and increasing unemployment and poverty is expressed in terms of a fear that crime or serious crime, violence, and drug use are now at epidemic levels or are out of control. Both popular media discussion and most social scientific research now accept that poverty and social inequality are on the increase (Fincher and Nieuwenhuysen 1998). Opinion makers talk about the emergence of a "seventy/thirty society" and the growth of an "underclass"— populations of the permanently unemployed, drug-abusing, homeless, sexually-promiscuous, criminally-inclined, and antisocial in the blighted outer suburbs of our cities. This idea is closely linked to allegations from what might be called a "conservative" perspective that the "welfare state" is creating a "welfare dependent culture."

Though our sympathies lie with the progressives in terms of our preference for more social investment by governments and better, more inclusive social programs, we are not inclined to simply assume that either the meaning or the veracity of these claims about homelessness, unemployment rates, or crime rates or the tendencies to create ghettos of the poor or the dispossessed are self-evidently true. That is, it is simply naive to think that these beliefs or fears simply reflect the "facts."[4] Our concern here, however, is not to enter into debate about these issues. Rather, our interest is in the way "risk talk" has helped to revive older discourses about "deviance" and "social pathology" and how these sustain governmental projects.

Talk about risk has been rendered "normal" and part of the contemporary common sense in social science disciplines including social work, sociology, the health sciences, psychology, criminology, and youth work. Talk of risk has also percolated into the human service professions working directly with individuals, families, and neighbourhoods. In these agencies the talk is of "risk indicators," "risk reduction," and "risk management." Indeed, one would find it difficult these days to find a government agency or community sector organisation working in human services that does not accept the concept of risk in their daily operations. Nor is it surprising that a relatively difficult book by the German social theorist Ulrich Beck called *Risk Society* (1992) should have become a best-seller.

How should we understand this idea of "risk," or the idea that there are people or population groups who are "at risk"? Should risk be understood simply as a consequence of empirical discovery made by social scientists trained in "objective" scientific methodology? How new is this research and the discourses of risk it depends upon? Should risk-based approaches, for example with social policy or crime control, be viewed as "progressive" or "conservative" interventions in the policy/practice field? What are some of the consequences of this way of thinking about social problems such as unemployment or crime?

In this book we argue that governments, policy makers, and the community at large need to think more deeply about a range of problems which have been sitting on the horizon of public anxiety for some time, and which are now thoroughly wrapped up in talk about risk. Because of the dominant role played by an empiricist research program in social sciences (with sociology, criminology, and economics) in both "discovering" problems and informing community debate, and with media reporting and policy responses, we need to think with and against some of the conventional ways the social sciences have constructed the kinds of problems we wish to discuss. In doing this we rely heavily, though not uncritically, on some of the work developed by writers such as Rose (1990) and Dean and Hindess (1998) in a dialogue with the French writer Michel Foucault about the theme of "government."

In this book we examine how the concept of "risk" has informed some recent research and policy formulation regarding problems affecting young people. We use the idea of "government" to do this and explore the ways the category of risk has been used to "redefine" policy responses to certain social problems in relation to the way various groups, including social scientists, politicians, and policy makers, and law enforcement agencies think about unemployment, crime, and homelessness. To do this we consider closely a number of important research projects including:

- Australian research on youth unemployment

- Australian and Canadian research on youth homelessness
- Australian and British research on juvenile crime and crime prevention

The studies we examine here are important examples of the risk-based discourse that underpins contemporary thinking about preventative strategies related to youth problems such as youth homelessness, unemployment, and juvenile crime. Yet the emergence of a risk-based, developmental approach to social problems has not attracted the kind of critical attention it deserves.

We argue that the discovery and research of "at-risk" populations is part of a long-running social science project of "government" in which experts and agencies explore ways of identifying and managing problem populations or even "preventing" certain "problem" activity. We suggest that this governmental project has been closely linked to the evolution of a "scientific" body of criminological and sociological research and theory, which for simplifying purposes we can refer to as "conventional" social science (read sociologists and criminologists).[5] Focusing on governmentality helps to gently undo the powerful symmetry long established between the conventional empiricist and broad-church positivist social science research program and the no less conventional understandings of policy-making processes. (This understanding is expressed, for example, in the "rational" [May and Wildavsky 1978] and the "incremental" [Lindblom 1959] models of policy, which complacently assume that policy making occurs in response to the "discovery" of "real problems".)

Conventional social scientists are concerned with "discovering" and measuring the incidence of given social problems such as unemployment, crime, or homelessness and then "explaining" why some people are at risk of falling into these states. This has been done by recourse to a wide variety of causal variables. Much conventional social science assumes that "crime," the "crime rate," and "unemployment" are objective facts, and these phenomena are types of behaviour or patterned social activities determined by a mixture of biological, psychological, and sociological factors. Conventional social scientists tend to assume that it is possible using models of proper, that is, epistemologically guaranteed, "scientific method" to discover the "causes" of the "crime rate" or the risk factors which predispose certain people to experience certain problems.

Much of the new discourse of risk builds on the canons of conventional social science research methods, while taking advantage of the recent recruitment of economic liberal values and ideas which are signified by the return of economic analysis and policy prescription in public policy making. That is, while "risk" has supplanted older categories such as "delinquency," "social pathology," the "criminal personality," and "maladjustment"—ideas that were foundational to criminology or to the sociology of deviance—the methodologies, assumptions, and politics of governance inherent in the older project of government remain the same.

In this way the evolution of risk talk simply perpetuates established ideas about criminality being the kind of behaviour in which the "the poor," "the unemployed," and "the underclass" engage. The "science of risk," to a large degree, continues the argument that crime is synonymous with, or caused by, "working-class people" or rogue elements of the "underclass." Recent and praised studies of Canadian "street kids," such as Hagan and McCarthy"s (1997) work and the Australian work of Chamberlain and MacKenzie (1998), stand in a long line of conventional sociology.

Although risk-based discourses have become popular among politicians and policy makers in recent years, the assumptions, ideas, methodologies, and politics underpinning them are far from new. The assumptions underpinning the modern risk discourse originate in some of the very earliest attempts by conventional sociologists and criminologists to identify and measure the "causes" of a range of social problems such as unemployment, broken families, "illicit" drug use, and crime.

At another level, however, risk-based approaches are part of newer kinds of governmental policies involving renewed attempts to control and regulate whole sections of the population, especially of young people who are potentially at risk of contributing to the "crime problem" and "the youth problem."

In chapter 1 we begin by discussing why a discourse and a "science of risk" have emerged recently, before outlining how we propose to use the category of government.

Notes

¹ See, for example, Robertson 1985; Bureau of Industry Economics 1989; Robertson 1992; Harris, 1993; Lloyd 1995; and Waters 1995.

² This leads in an unfortunate way to some hyperbolic claims such as Mark Latham's (1998) that "the dichotomy constructed last century between labour and capital has gradually lost its pertinence through...this century," a claim based on his technological-determinist views about the rise of the information age.

³ See, for example, Emy 1993; Castles, Gerritsen, and Vowles 1996; Catley 1996; Latham 1998; and Tanner 1999.

⁴ As we suggest later there is no valid reason to accept the proposition that "empirical" research about things such as "crime rates" is credible because it reports in an "objective" fashion what is said to be actually "there" (Holloway and Jefferson 1997: 258). In short, there are questions about how people or whole communities come to "know" there is a "social problem."

⁵ In constructing this account, we are NOT saying that all sociologists or criminologists are "conventional" practitioners of their discipline. These disciplines have always contained "oppositional" tendencies.

Chapter One: The Discovery of Risk and the Governmental Project

We must remember that, however much society may have changed for the better, the lowest stratum of all has not changed, and that lawlessness, cupidity and ruffianism are just as rife in it now as they were in the days of Sir Robert Walpole..."We see by what a very thin and precarious partition after all we are divided from the elements of violence which underlie all civilised societies.
(Blackwood Magazine, 1893)

Talk about risk has become increasingly central to much human service intervention and also to associated social science disciplines, including sociology, psychology, criminology, youth work, and social work.[1] Many social scientists now spend their time measuring the levels of social and personal risk which are indicated by poverty, disadvantage, unemployment, low income, poor health and housing, bad schooling, family dysfunction, personality deficit, and so forth. Risk has also figured prominently in the policies and practices of many education and training "industries."[2]

In social science disciplines the idea of risk in relationship to issues such as unemployment, homelessness, or the "crime rate" is coming close to achieving commonsense status. That status notwithstanding, questions need to be asked. How should we think about this idea of "risk"? How should we think about the claim that there are people or population groups who are "at risk"? Should risk be understood simply as a consequence of empirical discovery by social scientists trained in "objective" scientific methodology? How new is this research and the discourse of risk it depends upon? What are some of the consequences of this way of thinking about social problems such as unemployment and crime? How should we relate this idea of risk to state-sponsored policy processes?

First, however, we ask what is the risk talk about and why did talk about risk begin to surface in the 1980s and 1990s?

Risk

For centuries the idea of risk was the preserve of gamblers. (The word "risk" comes from the Renaissance Italian *risicare*, meaning "to dare.") From the eighteenth to the twentieth centuries, first actuaries associated with the insurance industry, and more recently emergency services, have made the concept of "risk" central to their professional calculations or interventions. It has even entered into the upper echelons of social theory.

Quite recently what we call "Risk I" (to distinguish it from "Risk II") has become a central metaphor used by contemporary social theorists to discuss the regulation of human affairs in "late modernity" (Beck 1992; Bernstein 1996; Kelly 1998; Lupton 1999).

In effect, the talk about "risk" is legitimated by the use of yet another idea, that is, "Risk Society," which sociologists and journalists especially seem to take exceptionally seriously. That some of the leading social theorists of our time are now preoccupied with the category of "Risk I" is meant to define the leading quality of an entire social order, that is, "Risk Society." "Risk II," on the other hand, belongs to a set of expert technologies designed to calculate the threat to personal development, social adjustment, or social order posed by specific risk factors. Because we are mostly interested in Risk II, we will not make much reference to the distinction after the next few pages.

"Risk Society"

Given the extraordinary importance attached to "social theory"—not least of all by its practitioners—it is perhaps not surprising that the idea of risk has segued out onto a broader intellectual and cultural stage. For this, Ulrich Beck has something to answer for.

Beck"s work (1992, 1998) contributes to one of the central themes of contemporary social theory and builds on a persistent interest among sociologists and theorists about how best to characterise societal development. Since August Comte, social theorists have been curious about how to define and describe the evolution of "modern society" (i.e., "modernity," "capitalism," "industrial society," etc.). Beck coined the idea of the "risk society" and thereby made his mark on this tradition. By "risk,"

Beck (1992) meant simply to suggest the kinds of anxiety or uncertainty posed by environmental catastrophe, the threat of nuclear war, or epidemic diseases such as AIDS. The notion of "risk society" also contributed to long-standing debates entered into by social theorists about how to identify the shift from "modernity" (or "industrial society" or...) to a "postmodern" (or "postindustrial condition" or...).

Beck (1992, 1998) and others, such as Giddens (1990) and Beck, Giddens, and Lash (1994), explain what is now happening by claiming it is part of a transition from one type of society ("classical," "modern," or "industrial" society) to another ("risk society," or "postindustrial," "postmodern" society). According to Beck, modern societies are in transition from being a "class society" to a "risk society." This, he says, means that modern societies are now passing from being "class-based" and concerned to distribute "socially produced wealth and related conflicts" (1992: 20) to becoming "risk-producing societies" where people have to address the consequences of excessive production, such as environmental hazards. This, however, is not all that can be said. The transition also involves, says Beck (1998: 9), the claim that "Society has become a laboratory where there is nobody in charge." (This might be news to governments, the armed forces, or some corporations, but we should never hold up a social theorist when they are in full flight by calling attention to too much reality.)

For Beck, a defining feature of our phase of modernity (what he calls "radicalised modernity") is that our society now produces a range of hazards and risks for which no one is actually responsible, and for which there are frequently no apparent explanations.

Within industrial society, risks were produced locally and there were appropriate respondents (i.e., the welfare state) which accepted responsibility for locally produced risks and dangers and which accepted collective responsibility through statutory protection and compensation for accidents, illness, or unemployment. Although Beck (1998: 17) focuses on the manufacture of ecological hazards, he indicates that the same mechanisms that produce ecological hazards are also producing "the disintegration of nuclear families, stable labour markets, segregated gender roles, [and] social classes."

These he identifies as the spread of new technologies, globalisation, and the marketisation of once public services. As he emphasises, these factors mean that nobody is in control, nobody is responsible. In other words, "Risk becomes another word for "nobody knows"" (Beck 1998: 12). What is left is recognition of the reality and the emotions involved in dealing with the new forms of "organised irresponsibility" through the use of the old schemes. According to Beck (1998: 16):

> ...the modes of determining and perceiving risk, attributing causality and allocating compensation have irreversibly broken down, throwing the function of bureaucracies, states, economies and science into question. Risks that were calculable under industrial society become incalculable and unpredictable in risk society.

As Beck argues, we confront a basic problem in our time. This problem has to do with the fact that most people operate with the belief that they can indeed interpret and explain what is happening by using traditional or "industrial" modes of understanding and categories which assume some institutional or social responsibility, when these categories and expectations have actually been rendered irrelevant.

The transition out of a modern industrial society involves the rise of an increasingly individualised society which can be seen in the demise of old institutions and the loss of the traditional institutions socialising power. As Beck explains:

> Risk society begins where tradition ends, when, in all spheres of life, we can no longer take traditional certainties for granted. The less we can rely on traditional securities, the more risk we have to negotiate....There is an important line of argument which connects the theory of risk society, in this context to the processes of individualisation in spheres of work, family life and self-identity (Beck 1998: 10).

According to Beck, the transition occurs in phases. In the first phase of the "risk society," Beck argues that society continues making "decisions and acts on the pattern of simple modernity" (Beck 1998: 17). For Beck, "risk society" is characterised by an increasing dependency on the individual along with a new social commitment to lifestyles and market mechanisms. Market competitive mechanisms rather than traditional ties are said to create greater risk as well as new modes of social integration. This shift in conditions of integration in conjunction with other changes such as the collapse of the youth labour market and general unemployment is of major significance to "youth." Among other things, this involves changing modes of integration where the competitive mechanisms of the market are increasingly determining the patterns and the rules of social life rather than the traditional ties (such as class, clan, family) (Beck 1992).

Ours is a time when some people question the promises of Enlightenment. Many are preoccupied with what they see as the apparent "irreversible" and "unstoppable" dynamics of globalisation. Beck appears to give aid and comfort to this sense of fashionable pessimism that is now associated by what some social theorists call "late modernity." Beck"s (1992) intervention bears hardly any connection to or with the avalanche of empirical social research which uses the idea of risk in an entirely different way. Yet in at least in one way the reception accorded to his idea of "risk society" might suggest something of the larger context of "elective affinities" that are at work.

In a general way, Beck"s work might be linked to the widespread loss of optimism and hope which Habermas pointed to when discussing the "exhaustion of utopian possibilities" in the 1980s following the collapse of Marxism as a theoretical project and the subsequent collapse of European communist states. Psychologists such as Tversky (1990: 75) concur, suggesting that the phenomenology of risk is coloured by pessimism: when people now take a risky decision in business or in other life-shaping decisions:

> There are a few things that would make you feel better, but the number of things that would make you feel worse is unbounded.

As Sennett (1999: 81) also notes now:

> ...risk taking is something other than the sunny reckoning of the possibilities contained in the present. The mathematics of risk offers no assurances.

Risk now embodies an anxiety that social order and personal well-being alike are under threat. van Swaaningen (1997: 174), for example, argues that the rise of a "risk society" discourse indicates:

> ...society [is] no longer oriented towards positive ideals but towards the negative ideal of limiting risk. Solidarity is no longer based on a positive feeling of connectedness but is expressed in a negative communality of fear.

We could ask when was "society" ever oriented to "positive ideals"—one where "solidarity rested on a positive feeling of connectedness"; van Swaaningen"s is a fantasy which may belong more to certain sociological discourses that identify "society" with a unitary "moral order" than to any actually existing historical society. Holloway and Jefferson (1997: 265) may be closer to the mark when they observe:

> In an age of uncertainty, discourses that appear to promise a resolution to ambivalence by providing identifiable victims and blamable villains, are likely to figure prominently in the State"s concerted attempts to impose social order.

We want to move on to consider the second way risk talk has come into prominence. This is the "Risk II" category which is used in an apparently "narrower" and far more "empirical" way in applied social research on social problems, young people, and policy making.

Risk Factors and Social Problems

What we call "Risk II" talk is the sort of talk which journalists like to use in headlines: "Dramatic new evidence that divorce increases the risk of "teen suicide"." Framing the problem of "risk" in this way produces the figure of "youth at risk." Talking in these ways leads to other talk about the "risk factors." Risk factors such as family status, heredity, socioeconomic circumstance, and psychological disposition are said to "cause" the problem which might include conventionally defined risks such as "crime," suicide, "delinquency," unemployment, drug use, sexual activity, violence, school-based activities, gang membership, computer hacking, graffiti, and so on.

It is no exaggeration to say that this has become a dominant way of thinking about and researching contemporary social problems. When it is applied to young people, risk talk has displaced the older talk about "delinquency." Peter Kelly (1998: 26), for example, reports that 2500 articles and conference papers alone have been written on the issue of "youth at risk" in the United States since 1989. Batten and Russell (1995) survey a parallel quantity of Australian risk research. Not surprisingly, this kind of talk has found its way into various policy fields. For example, it underpinned much of the Finn Report (Tait 1993), which examined the post-compulsory education and training from the perspective of employability (see also Bessant 1988; Marginson 1997: 175). As Kelly (1998: 33) notes:

> The discourse of youth-at-risk mobilises a form of probabilistic thinking, about certain preferred or ideal Adult futures, and the present behaviours and dispositions of Youth. This sort of probabilistic thinking attempts to construct statistically valid, causal relationships between these different configurations.

Although this is to anticipate our argument, we will argue that this talk about "risk" and the way it sanctions the use of numbers to convey an impression of precision, objectivity, and credibility is at best highly ambiguous, and at worst highly problematic. Whatever is meant by "risk," it, like so many forms of action or emotion, does NOT have any obvious empirical qualities.

It is in fact very much a quality produced or manufactured by calculation and measurement. Whether the measurements or calculations are about unambiguously "real things" (such as chairs, dogs, or mountains) or metric entities conjured up by the researcher by means of what is called "operationalisation" is another question entirely. As Douglas (1974: 30) explains:

> How much risk [there is] is a matter for the experts, but it is taken for granted that the matter is ascertainable. Anyone who insists there is a high degree of uncertainty is taken to be opting out of accountability.

As Douglas (1974: 42) observes, the concept of risk endeavours "to turn uncertainties into possibilities." The calibration of risk, therefore, becomes a professional activity conducted by accredited experts in the "war against chaos" in the continuing "battle for order" (Bauman 1991: 11). Risk talk suggests that social problems have an objective, value-free status and encourages the no less naive yet seductive and dangerous idea that technical fixes can be developed by experts to "treat" any human ailment or social condition.

"Risk talk" has arisen recently because the phenomena it refers to are "actually" there. Contrary to this naive suggestion, we would rather suggest that there are complex social and intellectual processes at work that enable some ideas to fill up the discursive space available.

Risk and Historical Decline?

Historians such as Pearson (1983) have shown how each generation believes itself uniquely threatened by the signs and symptoms of degeneration often signified by concerns about criminals, rising crime rates, and the threat of "hooligans." Should we see the present talk of risk and young people as simply the latest expression of a long tradition of fear and anxiety, a tendency that is somehow wired into history? We do not believe this is a particularly helpful approach.

For example, could it be argued that the contemporary emphasis on risk indicates that our lives, either personally or collectively, are now either less secure or less oriented to hopeful outlooks than at any other point in history? It may be, however, difficult if not impossible to establish a rational basis for evaluating this. (Historians such as Herman [1997] point out that cultural pessimism is far from being a condition unique to Western societies at the end of the twentieth century; after all, Athenians [in the sixth century B.C.] had their complex tales of decline from a Golden Age). There is little point trying to establish a rational basis for whether such a belief does or does not exist. As W. I. Thomas noted at the end of the 1920s, however real they are (or not), ideas are real in their consequences. There are now sufficient numbers of people talking about risk to make these ideas consequential.

We cannot, however, draw too many conclusions from the fact that cultural pessimism has a long history. Pick (1993: 18) argues that insisting on the ways adults have groaned about young people"s wicked ways since Socrates complained about Athenian youth can produce a paradox:

> On the one hand it alerts us to the relativity of such absolute claims and discloses their place in a much longer series of commentaries. On the other hand it too easily suppresses historical difference by petrifying discourses into apparently unchanging age-old mythologies—hooligans, bread and circuses, degeneration.

Pick (1993: 18) continues:

> ...when studied closely within historical limits, important and revealing differences do emerge in the meaning of seemingly homogenous and timeless concepts.

There may be more than a coincidence operating in the fact that the modern talk of risk has emerged at a time when both Australian public policy and "public culture" (informed and sustained by the mass media) have been powerfully reshaped by a resurgence of liberal individualism. Without reducing the emergence of talk about risk to a simple expression of resurgent liberalism, it seems there are some elective affinities between the two. Resurgent liberalism takes its form variously in a near-hegemonic policy discourse grounded in neoclassical economics, preoccupied with individual choices and freedoms and intent on reworking activities in the public sector via market-based activities and metaphors.

Promotion of a Third Way politics within Australian and British Labour parties (Latham 1998; Scott 2000) also takes its cue from attempts by Sen (1992) to rework a traditional social-democratic interest in equality by emphasising individual "social capabilities." The actuarial tendencies of economic liberalism which equate rationality with calculation are paralleled in social scientific research which calibrates risk factors and which claims to predict the degree to which a particular kind of person is "at risk."

- The risk discourse displays a powerful elective-affinity with the renewal of an entrepreneurial culture where risk taking has many positive associations. Since the 1980s, business takeovers, the amassing of vast fortunes, and the rise of new business heroes in the Bill Gates mold have all received sustained attention in the popular culture of Western societies. Equally, yet paradoxically, the risk discourse is also sustained by persistent public concern about "globalisation" and the social and economic consequences of unrestrained market forces, where a discourse of "risk" generates a new lexicon for representing old problems such as poverty, crime, unemployment, and homelessness.

- The discourse of risk offers governments in general, and the apparatus of criminal justice administration in particular, the opportunity to revitalise older practices of government (in the Foucauldian sense) which take advantage of the resurgence of economic liberalism and its individualism to promote new styles of policy.
- Finally, and within this larger setting, the risk discourse offers social sciences such as modernist criminology the opportunity to revitalise its long-standing commitment to an "empiricist" social research tradition.[3]

This is achieved partly by identifying the various "causes of crime" that render some individuals and social groups as more "at risk" than others. The next step is to engage the experts so that the differential risk factors can be isolated and ameliorative measures put in place. It is in this way that talk of risk is tied to contemporary governmental projects.

The Idea of Government

While the older sociology of deviance presumed the existence of a stable social and moral order called "society," the science of risk assumes the normality of restructuring, change, and the "death of the nation-state" in the wake of globalisation. Framing a macrosociology of "late modernity" poses challenges for those with a traditional interest in the government of social problems such as crime. Yet, as Beck (1992) argues, at the least, a discourse of risk holds out the prospect that within an era of globalisation, people or states can still try to manage the multiplicity of risks they now confront (see also Beck 1999).

In this way, as Mitchell Dean (1999: 131) insists, the idea of "risk" is central to "government":

> There is no such thing as risk in reality. Risk is a way—or rather a set of different ways—of ordering reality, of rendering it into a calculable form. It is a way of representing events so they might be made governable....It is a component of diverse forms of calculative rationality for governing the conduct of individuals, collectivities and populations.

While we think this is quite accurate as a characterisation, Dean is open to the criticism of allowing us to form the impression that the kind of risk talk we are interested in has been around for a long time, when this is not the case. There is still the question of history: Why have these particular kinds of ways of talking about social problems emerged at this time? The "sociology of risk" becomes a new way of framing old problems while reinvigorating old projects of governance. It is in this way that a long-standing governmentality project has been able to take on fresh life via the "science of risk."

Since the late 1970s, the work of Michel Foucault (1991) has helped shape new ways of thinking about the discovery of social problems and the development of public policy. Rather than assuming that social problems such as "crime," "homelessness," or "unemployment" have a self-evident facticity, or that their discovery is simply the automatic response of "society" to threats to "its" social control functions, or that their discovery represents the ideological effect of some social-structural interest (exercised by the middle class or by the patriarchal power of men), Foucault suggests that we discover what kinds of experts are involved in the construction of problems and the people who are problems. In this way Foucault sponsored an approach to research and scholarship around the ideas of "government" and "governmentality."[4] For our discussion, though, what do these words mean?

Although there is a lot of animated discussion about how best to characterise the idea of "government," people who do so argue that in our kind of society there is a long-standing and continuing attempt to regulate the conduct of the whole population (or parts of the population) by some of the people who make up that population (Rose 1994). The idea of "government" as developed by Foucault and those influenced by his work is not just about what "states" or governments do. As Dean and Hindess (1998: 2–3) have also noted, the idea of government is not just about what the state does or the political party institutions do. While the idea of government can refer to what the Blair or the Howard governments do, it also addresses every kind of attempt to govern the conduct of other people. "Government" is the regulation by some people of other people"s behaviour. As Dean and Hindess (1998: 2–3) say, "government is the conduct of conduct":

> In its most general sense, government is the conduct of conduct, where [this] refers to the manner in which individuals, groups and organisations manage their own behaviour. The conduct to be governed

may be one"s own or that of others: of the members of a household or of larger collectivities such as the population of a local community or a state. The government of a state may be conducted by agencies of the state...known collectively as the government...but it may also involve agencies of other kinds.

Some of this relates to what "the state" or "the government" does through its laws, its armies, police, courts, and judges. Much of it relates to the daily work of parents, religious people, social workers, teachers, doctors, advertising people, and journalists. Some governmentality is about "law and order" and much of it relates to books, films, newspaper articles, or professional advice offering a variety of information and "rules" for doing everything from dieting, exercising, having sex, building self-esteem, or acquiring a vocational skill, to choosing a holiday destination, raising children, or grieving properly. Some governmentality targets special populations such as "the poor," "young people," or "the criminal class," and some of it is almost universal in its scope.

Government, in short, refers to a loose amalgam of objectives (such as crime control or crime prevention), techniques of social investigation (such as empirical social scientific surveys or census taking), and an array of policies, institutions, and practices directed to the constant care, control, and "betterment" of problem populations or of the entire population (such as compulsory schooling or compulsory X-rays for disease control).

In a related way, the idea of "governmentality" can be used to refer to the knowledges and habits of thought that permit people to govern others or even themselves (Watts 1993/4). Minson (1993: 60), for example, argues that governmentality

> ...signifies a general form of organised reasoning, embracing practical ways of posing and addressing social and economic problems.

As Foucault argued, the social sciences and disciplines such as psychology, sociology, criminology, and economics played a key role in helping to inform a wide range of governmental projects.

This is especially pertinent given the kinds of tasks involved in the larger project of government. As Dean and Hindess (1998) point out, government involves at least four kinds of distinctive activity oriented to the "conduct of conduct."

They include first the study of problematisations, which asks how the activity of governing establishes the attributes of those who govern and/or of those who are being governed and the qualities of the problem being identified. Second, the study of government asks questions about the social or institutional site of the problematisation process. Third, the study of government does not assume that problems exist in themselves, but rather that they must be constituted through particular forms of reasoning. Finally, the study of modes of government identifies the formation and shaping of the identities, capacities, and statuses of members of the population—in this case of young people. (We discuss these processes at length in chapter 4).

In the twentieth century, criminology, along with the other social sciences, played a central role in various governmental projects, including those emanating from modern state-based agencies, as well as those coming from other social sectors such as community organisations, business companies, churches, the media and advertising industries, and a range of human service professionals. The risk category and risk analysis have become central to social research, theory, and policy making in Australia and in many other "Western" countries. "Youth at risk" appears to now enjoy a commonsense status in the many Western policy communities. Over the next chapters we explore three instances in which the idea of risk has come to take on a central significance. In the next chapter we look at the way modern social science approaches the problem of unemployment and how it frames it in terms of "risk."

Government and Risk: Thinking about Social Problems

The interest in "governmentality" and its role in developing "policy" is still new and underdeveloped in Australia, notwithstanding, for example, the work of Hunter (1988), Slee and Knight (1992), Dean (1994), and Dean and Hindess (1998). Perhaps this is why the category of risk is yet to be properly appreciated or treated within the governmentality literature.

However, given that we are writing primarily for people who are more likely to be interested in the question of crime, homelessness, and unemployment and less likely to be interested in the issues dealt with by the governmentality tradition, we will not spend much time exploring it in the abstract. We will, however, use some of the key ideas associated with the idea that social problems such as homelessness, unemployment, and crime are connected to issues of "government" to develop our arguments about how we should think about social problems and policies.

Establishing how the conduct of conduct is possible is the central concern of a growing body of research and theory that shelters under the umbrella of "government studies." Those engaged in this field of study do not seek to contribute to the (naive) analysis of the reality of, for example, "youth crime," which more "empirically" oriented researchers seek to undertake. In this chapter we critically review the role played by "risk" in recent modernist criminological research projects oriented to developing new modes of governing juvenile crime. The study of government addresses three interrelated processes (Dean and Hindess 1998: 8–13).

First, there is *the study of problematisations*. The concept of "problematisation"—a truly ugly new word—refers to the ways the activity of governing establishes the attributes of those who are being governed and the attributes of the problem being identified. For example, the 1996 massacre at Port Arthur in Tasmania provoked a volume of discussion about the kind of person who would do such a thing in terms of issues about the personality or the mental state of a mass killer, as well as the other kinds of people and institutions that allowed it to happen, including the conduct of state and federal governments (e.g., in regard to gun-ownership laws). In both cases the discussion goes to the concept of "government of conduct."

In this case the emergent science of risk can be considered as an example of one attempt, among many, to problematise the lifestyles of selected populations or their disposition to be subject to unemployment, homelessness, or to engage in misconduct. That is, the study of modes of government *identifies the formation and shaping of the identities, capacities, and statuses of members of the population*—in this case of young people. This is often the prelude to attempts to shape or reshape the identities of those whose conduct is to be governed. As we will show here, the question of identity is muffled by exponents of the science of risk; equally in regard to young people, they have long been a central target for pastoral care on the part of those with professional, legal, or vocational interests.

Second, the study of government raises questions about *the social or institutional site of the problematisation process* and addresses, for example, the difficulties facing an authority given a set of tasks rather than the application of a given set of general principles. In this regard the science of risk can be understood as one style, among many, of response to a variety of social problems.

There are many potential questions about the *social or institutional site of the problematisation process*. The evolution of a science of risk in contemporary criminology largely reflects a movement taking place inside academic institutions and policy units of the state.

What this means has been explained by David Garland (1994), who also offers a fruitful way of (re)writing the history of criminology. For Garland (1994), the trajectory of criminology involves the coevolution of "criminology" in terms of two logics of development that he has called a "governmental project" and a "science of causes," or what he calls the "Lombrosian project." Criminology, as a conventional enterprise, equals the Governmental Project plus the Lombrosian Science of Causes.

According to Garland, modern criminology continues to manifest aspects of both projects, revealing a continuing commitment to the Enlightenment faith in its Reason and in a reliance on the collection of scientific data to inform the project of government. As Garland (1994: 18) explains:

> By a "governmental project" I mean...the long series of empirical inquiries which since the eighteenth century have sought to enhance the efficient and equitable administration of justice by charting the patterns of crime and monitoring the practice of police and prisons.

This task, which evolves, for example, as a central part of the *state-istical movement* in the nineteenth century, saw the increasing use of fact-gathering techniques designed to catch the essential features of a wide range of "problem populations" (or the "criminal classes"). This continues to be a central characteristic of modern criminology and of in-house police and civil service research units and academic research centres that regularly produce statistics on crime and justice.

So, too, is "the Lombrosian tradition" which is a

> ...form of inquiry which aims to develop an aetiological, explanatory science based on the premise that criminals can somehow be differentiated from non-criminals (Garland 1994: 18).

Garland here is referring to the work of Cesare Lombroso (1836–1909), who produced a famous positivist study called *The Criminal* in 1876. Lombroso"s brand of "positivist scientism," yoked to a crude racial and class-based schema, provoked a flood-tide of parallel attempts to construct accounts of "the criminal" as well as a "science of causes" of criminal conduct. By the 1890s Gabriel Tarde (1843–1904), while heavily critical of Lombroso"s thesis, established the modernist synthesis which combined a criminological "science of causes" by drawing on social sciences such as sociology and psychology while working often quite pragmatically in the service of a governmental project which worked with "commonsense prejudices and political imperatives."

The result is modern criminology, a tension-filled field of study, teaching, and research caught between an ambitious "science of causes" and a more pragmatic, policy-oriented administrative project seeking to use science in the task of managing and controlling refractory population groups.

Finally, the study of government occurs because it does not assume that problems exist in themselves and pays attention to the ways problems must be constituted and *therefore pays attention to particular styles of reasoning* or what was once called "rhetoric." As Dean and Hindess (1998: 9) note:

> Problems become known through grids of evaluation and judgement about objects that are far from self-evident. The study of government thus entails the study of modes of reasoning.

In the emerging science of risk, there are particular styles of cognition which "discover" problems in particular ways.

Our "data" is a series of exemplary reports and research projects which have begun to constitute the science of risk as it is applied to problems such as unemployment, homelessness, and juvenile crime. Produced in the 1990s, these reports provide a useful basis for assessing the discursive emphasis on risk, especially with a view to identifying the critical silences and gaps in much contemporary criminological discourse. Our analysis suggests that notwithstanding the frequent affirmation by the authors of these reports of their "progressive" orientation to social policy or to criminal justice policy, their research and policy recommendations sit comfortably within the conventional social science tradition.

We turn now to another possible explanation for the rise of risk talk in our time.

Economic Liberalism and Risk

Ours is a period characterised by the near-hegemony, in political and cultural terms, of economic liberalism. In such a period, what kind of theory of deviance can we expect to find? One answer would be a "science of risk."

The resurgence of economic liberalism (or the theory and practice of public policy informed by neoclassical economics since the mid-1970s) has not just been about the refashioning of economic policy. It has also involved major shifts in the framing of the boundaries between "state" and "civil society" (Cerny 1991). It has seen the reworking of traditional meanings ascribed to the dichotomies "Left" and "Right" (Giddens 1995). This process of economic "reconstruction" has seen a fundamental redesign of Australian institutions and policies (Bell 1997). This includes "new" discourses and practices developed to subordinate a diversity of social value systems to economic needs which stress characteristics such as "trade liberalisation," "privatisation," and labour market "flexibility."

It has also helped reconstitute the conception of a "public" and of the idea of "society" as a discursively constituted social and moral order involving what Yeatman (1998: 227—41) calls the renewal of liberal individualism, owing much to what she calls "contractualism." (As Yeatman argues, some of these processes conform to the worst expectations of left critics of economic liberalism, while others point to new kinds of post-patrimonial egalitarian politics.)

In an era of resurgent economic liberalism, talk of risk is combined with the language of competition, business, and the market, along with a variety of doctrines espousing "mutual responsibility" and "self determination." These terms are used variously to define the ethics and the type of relationship a young person should have with themselves, their family, and community. The morality of entrepreneurship, for example, is aimed at the subjectivity of the young person; thus, we see within discourses about risk an emphasis on self-reliance, personal responsibility, and autonomy.

We can see these effects operating in the rise of the science of "risk." Much of this science of risk depends on the central figure in liberal theory, the individual.

The mainstream of classical liberal theory and subsets of that theory such as neoclassical economics depend on the following claims (Arblaster 1984: 1–48). The first is the ontological claim that individuals are the only entities in the social world that matter and that they are ontologically prior to "society." In other words, only individuals can have preferences, choices, or values or take decisions and engage in actions. In the 1980s British Prime Minister Margaret Thatcher gave voice to this view when she opined: "There is no such thing as society." The second main claim in classical liberal theory is epistemological. It is argued that only theories grounded in "methodological individualism" can accurately chart the activities of individuals and the ways individual choices constitute collectivities, institutions, or society itself.

According to this new version of neoclassical economic liberal worldview:

1. "Individuals" have market attributes. They either have "enterprise" (energy, skills, and human/intellectual or economic capital) or they have deficits (a lack of skills, low intelligence, or inadequate capital). Individuals take their enterprise or deficits to "the market," where they calculate in a rational and strategic way what actions will best promote their happiness in competition with other like individuals (see Elster [1986] for an extremely sophisticated discussion of the rational action model).
2. "Social institutions" are entities grounded in the activities of the individuals who constitute them. All institutions, especially those connected to "the state," are seen to be rigid. Moreover, they allegedly inhibit and obstruct individual choice, and this is damaging to the proper running of the marketplace. Social institutions do this because they are inefficient, costly, cumbersome, and bureaucratic, and they therefore distort the rational and happiness-oriented market interactions of individuals.

3. "Markets" provide the social framework in which individual energy, rationality, initiative, skill, and risk-taking enterprise can flourish. This, however, can only happen if they are kept free of institutional and state rigidities that obstruct the rationality of the market.

Metaphors such as "markets," "enterprise," "competition," "flexibility," and "individual" provide the primary categories which have informed the remaking of political talk and public policy in Australia and most Western countries since the early 1980s.

This neoliberal worldview and accompanying "reform agenda" have been accompanied by a growing ""public" anxiety about crime (Rose 1994). As David Garland (1996) notes, the United Kingdom has, since the early 1980s, seen the elevation of an "ever-increasing crime rate" as a basic "social fact." This has been accompanied by a rise in "victimology" and a growing disenchantment with the ability of the police to manage "law and order problems." In America, the United Kingdom, and Australia, an attack on the alleged "culture of welfare dependency" created by "Big Government," and specifically the "welfare state," has generated considerable discussion about the threat posed by "the unemployed," "the underclass," and the collapse of the "traditional family" and "traditional" social values (Abbott and Wallace 1989; Bessant 1995; Hil 1996).

Castells (1996, 1998) has little doubt that these societies are moving toward a "postindustrial" society. This shift can be characterised in terms of a decline within these societies of the traditional manufacturing industries and the rise of information and service industries. This shift has been accompanied by permanent mass unemployment and a heavy increase in unsecured employment. Governments have played an active role in what has been called the "globalisation" process by deregulating the labour market, freeing up controls on the finance sector, and introducing more targeted and conditional welfare benefits. Courtesy of the discourse of markets and privatisation measures, governments at all levels have contributed to a process of disinvestment in jobs (Boreham, Dow, and Leet 1999).

It is not surprising, given that "economic liberalism" rests on a version of "methodological individualism," that there has been a resurrection of older models of identifying and treating social problems as expressions of individual deficiency or pathology. In Australia, for example, official acceptance (Cass 1988) of the Organisation for Economic Cooperation and Development"s "active society" model since the late 1980s has resulted in the complete reform of the social security system (Gass 1988; OECD 1988). (Among its effects has been the increasing use of case management in employment services and labour market programs directed at remedying what are said to be the individual deficiencies in skill, motivation, or aptitude that "explain" why some people are unemployed.)

In the contemporary evolution of a science of risk, we frequently see two quite traditional intellectual movements operating in the history both of liberal social theory and of social scientific research. On the one hand, there is a movement to relocate the idea of risk away from the risk-taking individual (the "entrepreneur") and toward the idea that "social order" or "society" is at risk. On the other hand, while preserving some of the underlying individualist elements of liberalism, there is a movement from a positive evaluation where risk (taking) is a cea ntral dynamic factor in capitalist economic growth, to the negative evaluation that risk (as in risky behaviour) threatens society itself. Needless to say, most of the risk research is not about risk-taking behaviours on the part of individuals; *it is about identifying and diagnosing the risk to social order posed by particular subsets of the population.* As we demonstrate later, some risk-based research is the "natural" expression of a methodological individualism that locates the causes of "social problems" such as "unemployment," "poverty," or "homelessness" fairly and squarely with the individual and the largely psychologically dominated body of developmental and life-cycle research.

In an affirmation of the continuing potency of liberal individualism, the identification of the risk factors enables researchers to locate the source of these problems in the biological or psychological dispositions of the individual as "delinquent" or "criminal." This is not to deny that risk research also allows for the play of "social factors" such as "family," "neighbourhood," or "the community," but invariably these social entities are represented as "dysfunctional," "antisocial," or deficient. This has the effect of seeming to confirm that this research has paid its proper obeisance to sociological explanations, while actually diminishing interest in the social processes that produce "crime" and its representations.

This happens by encouraging the unreflective idea that "crime" is an objective correlate of personal, biological, or social dysfunction. A stress on the alleged objectivity, for example, of crime data means that crime is not understood either as the representations that constitute the "crime problem" or as the large range of criminal activity of which only that part done by "poor," black, or "working-class" people is defined as "crime."[5]

One unintended effect of the mainstream social research process is to deflect attention away from the social processes of governance—processes which include the discovery of social problems such as crime and the identification of its perpetrators. The logic of risk-based research establishes a way of understanding "the problem" that *excludes the roles and responsibilities of the more powerful groups involved in the government of crime and instead frames "the problem" as one identified at the level of individual analysis,* or as one involving individual responsibility, albeit only among a certain part of the population.

Notes

[1] See, for example, White 1989, 1994a, 1994b, 1995; Homel et al.; Potas, Vining and Wildon 1990; Eckersley 1988, 1992, 1993; Allat and Yeandle 1992; Chamberlain and MacKenzie 1998.

[2] See, for example, Abbott-Chapman and Patterson 1990; Ainley, Batten, and Miller 1984; Anderson 1979; Australian Curriculum Studies Association 1996; Australian Education Council Review Committee 1991; Batten and Russell 1995; Batten et al. 1991; Bradley 1992; Constable and Burton 1993; Sweet 1998; Wooden 1998; Hawkins, Arthur, and Catalano 1995; Chamberlain and MacKenzie 1998; and Hawkins et al. 1998.

[3] The new "science of risk" may play some part in enhancing the career prospects of those social scientists eager to demonstrate their "practicality" and "relevance" to the project of governance in a higher education setting where chasing research grants and demonstrating relevance have become important parts of the new managerial university. Equally, there is nothing especially new about the linking of personal careers and particular discursive fashions.

[4] See variously Hacking 1986; Rose 1989; Burchell, Gordon, and Miller 1991; Watts 1993/4; Dean and Hindess 1998.

[5] Crimes by governments which far outweigh ordinary crime in the twentieth century are almost a conceptual impossibility within criminology; "white-collar crime" is not a common object of criminological concern (if the amount of research literature devoted to it is any indication), while environmental crimes by corporates, for example, are usually redefined as "accidents."

Chapter Two: At Risk of Unemployment

74.6% of sociology is bunk.
(The Economist : 1995)

In 1998 the Howard Liberal-National Coalition Government introduced changes to Australia"s income support for young people in a unified and means-tested system known as the Common Youth Allowance. The justification for this "reform" was to better meet the needs of "at-risk" young people. The evolution of the "youth at risk" category—and more recently the addition of the "youth potentially at risk" category—followed mounting popular anxiety about youth unemployment.

It is plain that we are experiencing the demise of institutions such as Wage-Work, once seen as critical integrative mechanisms. If this assessment is accurate, it raises major questions about the future of social cohesion and how we can ensure young people can have access to generally accepted values and modes of social practice such as paid employment.

According to one dominant account of employment and adolescent adjustment, waged work provides an important medium for regulating young people, for structuring their time and identity. Young people without work are problematic because they lack an occupation to organise their daily lives. This work also depends on specific meta-narratives about the lifecycle. Notions of transition, integration, adjustment (to the "adult role"), and the very concept of "adolescence" are integral to the work of many intellectually trained professionals concerned about "youth at risk of unemployment." Historically, paid employment has been seen as functional in terms of providing the basis for social integration and a secure transition along that "precarious road" from the childlike adolescence to "the responsibilities" of adulthood.

The increase in youth unemployment since the 1970s has been disruptive to older processes which secured a transition to adulthood. If employment brings order, stability, and security, then unemployment delivers disorder and insecurity. Throughout the twentieth century, full-time waged work structured the lives of many young Australians, while joblessness was widely recognised as disruptive to the predictable patterns and transitionary phases young people were expected to pass through on the path to adulthood. With the concept of full-time waged work, this transition to adulthood has been seen as relatively secure and fixed. Without paid employment and financial independence, the various "stages" and events that mark out one"s progress in becoming adult (such as marriage and social autonomy) are seen as having been suspended and disrupted.

From the mid-1970s when evidence of the effects of youth unemployment began to gather, young people began to be represented as "victims" of unemployment and restructuring; by the mid-1990s it had become fashionable to blame "globalisation." This victim status heightened popular concern about "rising" rates of juvenile crime, suicide, homelessness, and substance abuse. As well as depicting "casualties of change" (Eckersley 1988, 1993), researchers and commentators have promoted the idea that they are graffiti artists, delinquents, gang members, or young offenders and as such are a menace to social order. The combination of unemployment and criminality has sustained the use of the metaphor of the "juvenile underclass" (White 1994a, 1994b; cf. Bessant 1995).

While the "at-risk" category can be treated as a consequence of large-scale social transformations, it mostly functions as an index of deficit usually located in the individual deemed to be "at risk." For commentators such as Eckersley, "youth at risk" are the "miner"s canaries" of our society in crisis, highly vulnerable to the "hazards of our time." The "at-risk" category signifies the "crisis" and apparently novel hazards and problems that characterise our era as dangerous, difficult, and crisis-ridden. According to Eckersley (1992: 18), these include

> ...pressures of increasing urbanisation, industrialisation, centralisation, mechanisation, individualisation, of growing populations, increasing global economic competition and accelerating change, of a strengthening material and economic domination of our lives and a weakening spiritual and moral influence (Eckersley 1992: 18).

As Kelly (1998: 22) points out, these features mirror Giddens" (1990) "risk profile of modernity." The restructuring of the labor market and economy coincided with the collapse of the full-time youth labor market that began in the 1980s (Wooden 1998: 35; Dryfoos 1990; Bell 1997; Langmore and Quiggin 1994; Quiggin 1996). The restructuring process has given rise to a range of specific anxieties about youth homelessness, youth suicide, juvenile delinquency, drug use, and addiction. The restructuring process has meant that "youth" encounter "new morbidities" that present major obstacles to becoming adults. Batten and Russell"s (1995: 1) position is typical:

> The term "at risk"...is used to describe or identify young people who, beset by particular difficulties and disadvantages, are thought likely to fail to achieve the development in their adolescent years that would provide a sound basis for a satisfying and fulfilling adult life.

In the context of our observations about the framework of government, we will use the issue of youth unemployment as a guide to *the study of problematisations*. That is, we ask how the activity of governing establishes the attributes of those who govern and/or of those who are being governed and the qualities of the problem being identified.

Youth at Risk

Much of this at-risk literature depends on "popular" and "social scientific" discourses about adolescence as a period in the lifecycle that

1. is inherently agonistic and
2. is concerned with making a transition from childhood to adulthood, which is in itself said to be a risk-ridden project.

Framing the problem of "risk" in this way produces the figure of "youth at risk" (Bessant 2000, 2001). It is an approach that is especially prevalent in the education/training industry, especially in relation to secondary students threatening not to complete Year 12 or its equivalent (see Australian Education Council Review Committee 1991; Coopers, Lybrand Consultants, and Ashden Milligan 1992; Australian Curriculum Studies Association 1992; DEET 1992; Batten et al. 1991; Bradley1992; Constable and Burton 1993; Batten and Russell 1995; Ward et al. 1998).

For most of the period of economic crisis since 1975, an "incomplete education" has been defined as the key factor that places the young person "at risk" of unemployment (Ainley, Batten, and Miller 1984; Dryfoos 1990, 1994, 1996; Bradley and Stock 1993; Dwyer 1997). For Meredith Edwards (1998: 25), the enormity of the problem of "youth at risk" by their opting out of education is apparent:

> A group of 20, perhaps 25 percent of young people are at risk, if you include those who might be in part-time education or part-time employment as well as those who are unemployed or out of the labour market.

An unfinished education is said to also place the young person "at risk" of other social ills such as psychological depression, juvenile crime, suicide, homelessness, and drug abuse. Those "at risk" of unemployment are students who either leave the education system "too early," or who show signs of leaving in the foreseeable future. From Freeland"s (1996) perspective, for example, unemployment relies on an analysis of ABS Labour Force statistics, which he argues can distinguish between those who are "gravely at risk" and the simply "at-risk" young person. His analysis is based on various factors such as whether the young person is in full-time schooling, whether they are unemployed, and whether they are in part-time employment. The idea that young people ought to remain within the education system has become so normative to the extent that the category of "youth at risk of unemployment" has achieved near commonsense status in the sector. Preventing young people from becoming unemployed has affected in significant ways the very character of our education institutions, so much so that the primary objectives of most institutions" "learning outcomes" appear to be directed toward the demand of the labour market (Marginson 1997).

Most of the at-risk literature depends on "popular" and "social scientific" discourses about adolescence as an inherently difficult time in the lifecycle. That is, adolescence involves making a transition from "childhood" to "adulthood," which is a risky project. Given this basic assumption, it is not surprising to find that the empirical and social scientific work on risk factors appears to set loose the potential for an almost limitless field of discovery of risk factors. As Batten and Withers (1995: 1) indicate, "modern scientific understandings" of the adolescent stage in the lifecycle mean that the psychological, biological, economic, and sociocultural factors are such that "*all youths are in some sense at risk*" (our emphasis). Batten and Russell underscore the reach of the category:

> ...there is not a "typical" at risk student, but a wide variety of young people of different needs and capacities, each of them exposed to different combinations of risk factors (Batten and Russell 1995: vii).

As a cursory survey of the risk literature indicates, the risk factors are almost unlimited. The factors that allegedly constitute "at-risk youth" extend from indicators of specific disadvantage (such as gender, aboriginality, or physical disability) to indicators that appear to be common to all fourteen-to-twenty-five-year-olds. Casting a net far enough to include all young people makes a corrective response not only a "necessity" but also a responsible solution; it sanctions any intervention as long as that response is justified in terms of "reducing" the risk factors.

Explaining Unemployment

There are some questions that now need to posed: How good is the "youth-at-risk" research literature at explaining problems such as unemployment? How do those explanations help answer the question as to why so many young people are now facing unemployment?

The persistence of unemployment within the context of the unequal distribution of paid work, involving overwork, underemployment, and unemployment, since the 1970s has generally been explained either by pointing to a set of structural constraints and dynamics which appear to be out of anyone"s control or else by pointing to alleged characteristics of the unemployed.

The shift from industrial to postindustrial society, which includes the spread of new technologies such as IT, is often used to suggest that what we are experiencing is structurally necessary and part of an irreversible process of "modernisation" or "globalisation" and that unemployment is one of the prices "we" all must pay for being present at a time of great change (e.g., Jones 1982; Catley 1996).

Equally among policy makers and many experts in countries such as Australia, the temptation to explain the persistence of unemployment in term of deficiencies found among the unemployed has proven irresistible. Certainly, most of the "at-risk" literature depends on a deficit model.

Deficits of the Unemployed?

Numerous researchers have offered explanations of youth unemployment which speak about the "deficits of the unemployed" in terms of skill, motivation, morality, character, level of education, or vocational training. Explanations of youth unemployment which claim that the young unemployed either "lack" certain qualities or else display certain "risk factors" here relied on the continuous use of a deficit model, which identifies lack of skills, job readiness, or motivation as the essential problem. (One reason frequently offered, especially in the 1980s, was that they had this deficit because of the failure of schools and universities to adequately prepare young people for the demands of waged work in the modern era (e.g., *Bulletin*, 10 February 1981: 28; Messel, *Australian*, 17 February 1978; Chipman, *Australian*, 3 February 1998; Manne and James). On the basis of this ""diagnosis," the "obvious" corrective step is to provide more education, more vocational training, and more targeted labour market programs.

Research supporting these descriptions of the youth unemployment problem has been extensively encouraged by governments. Defining the problem as a "problem of the unemployed" has been successfully represented since the mid-1970s as an answer to the unemployment problem; it has underpinned the defence of various labour market programs, and of the vocational educational policies. It has also been useful for dealing with difficult questions confronting mainstream economic theory. This is also the least useful and quite often the most damaging heuristic framework. Its use seems predominantly ideological. In other words, it is used to deflect criticism or to move attention from more appropriate factors.

Neoclassical economists have constituted both the problem of unemployment and the national economic policy established to address it. Representative economists (and even "progressive" economists such as Gregory [1997: 53—74]) have explained Australia"s experience of unemployment in terms of

- excessive domestic wages or wage increases
- rigidities in the labour market reinforced by unions and/or an "inflexible" industrial relations system
- business cycle downturns
- international trade and price pressures

According to advocates of mainstream economic theory, high levels of economic growth (measured by increases in GDP) must produce increased employment and therefore solve the problem of unemployment. Yet Australia, along with other OECD countries, has seen the coexistence of high unemployment *and* high levels of economic growth. As Table 2.1 below indicates, such claims are unsustainable: As company profits increase, rates of unemployment have not declined.

Table 2.1: Relationship between Corporate Gross Surplus and Unemployment 1990—97

	Corporate Gross Operating Surplus Annual Average (%)	Unemployment Rate Annual Average (%)
1990—91	14.6	8.3
1991—92	14.8	10.3
1992—93	15.7	10.9
1993—94	16.5	10.5
1994—95	16.3	8.9
1995—96	16.8	8.4
1996—97	16.3	8.3

(Source: ABS, Australian Economic Indicators, 1350.0 September 1998: 27 and 86)

Despite this situation, many economists support the proposition that it is a lack of vocational or personal skills on the part of the unemployed, or of those "at risk of unemployment," which best explains the persistence of high rates of unemployment. Thus, DEET (1995: 6) argued that the

> ...erosion of skills of the unemployed and loss of motivation reducing their attractiveness to employers best explain this problem. Governments have taken comfort from this "finding."

Governments have also used public concern about "dole bludgers" mobilised by media personalities to enlist the support of some sections of the welfare industry and the community generally, which have long been accustomed to "victim-blaming" discourses (Ryan 1976). The constitution of an Australian unemployment policy has taken the form of a preoccupation with making policy for the unemployed. This has relied on a deficit model account of the "unemployed" which identifies "their" lack of skills, job readiness, flexibility, or motivation as the essential problems for which labour market programs are the most appropriate response. In this way they have drawn on the methodological individualism of conventional or neoclassical economics.

The neoclassical tradition (and its particular expression in "labour market theory") produces an insistent preoccupation with the alleged individual capacities, dispositions, and deficits of the job seeker (or of "the unemployed"). This preoccupation is an organic expression of the methodological and ontological "individualism" of the neoclassical tradition. This has meant that representative neoclassical economists (and even "progressive" economists such as Gregory [1997: 223—24]) frequently conclude their analysis of the unemployment problem by converting it into a problem of the unemployed.

The neoclassical tradition has always assumed the centrality of the market. Neoclassical economists have long been accustomed to analysing the market as if it were simply the sum of individual decisions taken by "rational economic actors" (as well as a small number of the factors said to influence the job seeker or employee"s capacity to get a job). In the neoclassical tradition, markets are made up of individuals who are driven by individual desires, who exercise their rationality, and deploy individual endowments, all the while exchanging commodities and services so as to maximise their own "utility" (or "happiness" or "welfare"). The antisocial prejudices of this tradition are writ large in the primacy it accords to ahistorical individual consumer choices and in the way it privileges a theoretical narrative about exchange relations between "individual" owners of resources (such as labour or capital). Simons" classic account of "income" is defined, for example, as the

> ...algebraic *sum* of (i) *the market value of rights exercised in consumption* and (ii) the change in the value of the store of property rights between the beginning and end of the period. (Simons 1938: 50) (our emphasis).

The entire edifice and the credibility of neoclassical economics depend on an asocial model of "rational economic man." In one stunning vindication of the continuing reliance of such analyses on the model of the rational, utility-maximising individual, Debelle and Vickery (1998: 249) assert that

> The labour supply or participation rate equation can be derived from an aggregate version of the individual"s labour/leisure choice in which labour supply is determined by the wage, the prices of goods in an individual"s consumption basket and non-wage income. An individual will supply labour, provided that the pay-off from accepting employment exceeds their reservation wage.

As Prychitko observes:

> ...neo-classical economics provides a formal theory of rational choice, which assumes away questions of ignorance and uncertainty (at best, agents are modelled under conditions of "risk" which collapses into a certainty equivalent), time (time is treated as a parameter rather than a flow of consciousness) and social-institutional change (at best economists engage in comparative statics, studying the movement from one equilibrium to another) (Prychitko 1995: 1).

Neoclassical economics rests its theoretical credibility on a version of methodological individualism—which Prychitko refers to as a "naive individualism." Each agent is an "isolate" with their preferences and constraints simply given. As EPAC (1995: 27) points out:

> A great part of economic, social and political analysis focuses on the role, responsibilities and rights of individuals...this makes sense as our society and economy are based on rights of individuals, and it is their behaviour which is important for how the economy and our society operates.

Personal relationships between economic agents are presumed not to exist, for if they did the system would possibly fail to achieve its optimal state; in this version, the individual merely reacts to the given state of the world; the meaning of the individual"s acts for the actor is ignored or obliterated. Yet, the individualism of the tradition can become alarmingly abstracted. When pressed, key figures have been prepared to ditch the actual ontologically and socially grounded person. Pareto puts it like this when he says that "the individual can disappear, provided he leaves us this photograph of his tastes" (1971/1927: 120). Hahn more recently is even more exemplary:

> Traditional equilibrium theory does best when the individual is of no importance—he is of measure zero. My theory also does best when all the given theoretical problems arising from the individuals mattering do not have to be taken into account (Hahn 1973: 330).

Individual dispositions, their desires, and attributes take on special significance given the centrality of the exchange relationship and the choices individuals make

> ...about the type of occupation they wish to pursue, whether they wish to pursue high incomes or job satisfaction or status...and between the amount of work and leisure they undertake. They are also able to exercise choices related to their time preferences (EPAC 1995: 23).

In the neoclassical tradition, there is no space for a theory of social classes, a theory of unequal power, or the actuality of social inequality.[1] There is also no interest in the actual plurality of social relationships or diverse logics of social action experienced by real people; the only "object of desire" is the strategic, egoistic, utility-maximising competitive individual. Individual outcomes and dispositions alone matter.

Those who work in this paradigm are discursively incapable of asking questions about the role and dispositions of those with the power of decision-making in terms of investment and job creation, either in the corporate business sector or in the public sector. This refusal is accompanied by an inability or an unwillingness to think carefully about the interconnections within any complex society that might shed a different light on certain commonsense "economic" claims.

It is not surprising then to find contemporary economists explaining persistent unemployment in individualistic terms. Economists, for example, have found it useful to argue that the

> ...erosion of skills of the unemployed and loss of motivation reducing their attractiveness to employers may explain the persistence of unemployment (DEET 1995: 6).

That this may say more about the need on the part of economists to resolve the cognitive dissonance confronting economists and their "theory" posed by the coexistence of high unemployment *and* high levels of economic growth cannot be disallowed. Whatever the reason, governments have been comforted by this "finding"; they have also not been slow to take advantage of public concern about "dole bludgers" — mobilised by ever-vigilant media personalities into recurrent "moral panics" — or conversely, to enlist the backing of the welfare industry long-wedded to "victim-blaming" discourses (Ryan 1976). Labour market programs have been the primary means whereby successive governments have reconstituted the problem represented by the persistent growth in the numbers of the unemployed. Redefining the problem as *the problem of the unemployed* has been successfully represented for the past decade or more as an answer to the unemployment problem.

Unemployment Risk Factors

Anh Le and Paul Miller (1999), two Australian econometricians, produced a methodologically sophisticated report for the Australian Bureau of Statistics (ABS). Le and Miller positioned themselves within a considerable body of empirical work which aimed to quantify the causal links between a variety of personal-attribute factors such as age, education attainment, language skills, birthplace, or region of residence, and employment outcomes. Their research project was designed to identify an "index of risk factors" associated with unemployment.

Le and Miller are not the first, nor are they the only, researchers inclined to develop a risk index for unemployment, nor are they the only ones to talk in term of risk factors and joblessness. In 1987, Miller and Volker produced a risk index that could be used to assess the probability of an individual"s unemployment. In this project the population was categorised into two groups: those at risk of unemployment and those not at risk. People with a personal history of unemployment, those with dependent family members, and early school leavers were said to be clearly at risk. This research also had policy implications: It meant that it could be used to target those specific groups (Miller and Volker 1987; see also Seth-Purdie 2001). As Le and Miller (1999) note, the research in this area, almost all of it the work of labour market economists working within the neoclassical framework, has focused

1. on those variables that affect labour market productivity outcomes,
2. on those factors that affect employment/unemployment outcomes, and/or on
3. the role played by previous labour market experience that affects unemployment.

Le and Miller clearly intend to categorise people according to their "risk of unemployment" as a prelude to informing policy making. They set out to ascertain the level of risk across four levels: "very high risk," "high risk," "medium risk," and "low risk." To do this they drew on a longitudinal research project, the Survey of Employment and Unemployment Patterns (SEUP), which collected data in two waves over three years (1995-97) from samples of people aged 15-59 put together from three groups (i.e., Jobseekers [N= 5488], Labour Market Programme participants [N=1019], and a Population Reference Group [N=2311], producing a total sample population of 8,818 persons).[2] Le and Miller produce a new set of estimates of the "determinants" that give the probability that someone will be unemployed. The data is used to produce sets of cross-tabulations that are then used for an examination of the relationships between labour market outcomes and a number of key characteristics such as age or gender.

To do this, Le and Miller applied many of the most impressive elements of contemporary social science statistical techniques, complete with an equation for unemployment. The first equation, equation A, reads as follows:
$U^* + X ... j j j$

Le and Miller note, for example, that U^*j is the propensity of an individual to become unemployed, whereas X refers to the causal variables smoothed statistically. To equation A are then added equation B, which is a logit model, and equation C, which uses "associated estimated coefficients," which are understood as approximations only. Each of the variables are then defined as "mutually dichotomous variables."

As a result of their analysis of the SEUP data (1995—97) and their formal analysis of the causal determinants of unemployment,

Le and Miller construct a "risk of unemployment index." This is based on their assessment that there are a "remarkable consistency" of labour market outcomes over time, which are correlated with the variables. The authors argue that the model of probability of unemployment shows that age, educational attainment, English proficiency, disability, and marital status are important determinants of the probability of being unemployed. Each of these identity markers are given a rating on a scale of employability. With education, for example, those with a tertiary or late-exit secondary school qualification are said to have an unemployment rate of between 6 and 10 percentage points less than those without such attributes. The age factor on the probability scale is said to be "relatively weak" (Le and Miller 1999: ix).

Estimates from the model of unemployment can then be used to categorise individuals according to their risk ("very high," "high risk," "medium risk," and "low risk"). This categorisation is based on two types of risk index. The first predicts the risk of unemployment using all the coefficients from the logit model. The second is an approximation of the first. Points are then given to "individual characteristics" in the same way the immigration system works (ix).

Their findings show that those at highest risk of unemployment are the low skilled, those with minimal English proficiency, people with disabilities, and the young. To demonstrate the accuracy of their model, the authors use the second wave of data collection (1995—96). They argue that:

> Those suggested as being at risk of unemployment in 1995 are shown to have inferior labour market performance during the second wave. They spent, on average, more time looking for work, they were also absent from the labour market for greater periods. Those results suggest that the risk index has merit. Moreover, examination of the performance of a risk index computed using a point system shows that this is a useable approach (x).

"Causal factors" are identified and linked to "predicted errors" to improve the forecasting capability of their model. They "found," for example, that a person is more likely to be without work if their family members are jobless. This revised model is said to show a "positive relationship" between the number of days a person looked for work in the year prior to the survey and their employment status.

"The relationship" between looking for work and current unemployment status produces what is noted as a "scar effect," or "inertia in labour market outcomes." The notion of a "scar effect" is a highly effective use of metaphor. It helps for example, to explain to their audience the problem of unemployment and cumulative disadvantage as if it were the product of an injury, or a defect caused by the person"s previous inability to secure waged work (xi). This means, say Le and Miller, that disadvantaged workers can be identified with a high degree of success, which from a policy point of view means, as they say, that the "targeting of skill enhancement assistance can be carried out if this is considered desirable."

A Critique

Although Le and Miller are working at an abstracted and highly sophisticated level, their findings in one sense should be neither controversial nor surprising to Australians already familiar with the broad outlines of the unemployment problem. Is it surprising, for example, to be told that young people are at higher-than-average-risk of unemployment, especially if they are also early school leavers, as are non-English-speaking people, older-age workers, or people with low levels of educational attainment? Given this, why then would we want to criticise this work? There are several grounds—some minor reasons and some more substantive reasons—for our concern.

First, there is the minor but surprising fault with some features of their population reference group which they themselves acknowledge to be somewhat odd. They pass surprisingly quickly over the embarrassment that their "representative" Population Reference Group sample is a peculiar representative sample. It has a mean age of 36, while two-thirds of its members are married, and one in five has a disability! The reader may also wonder on other grounds about the value of the findings in relation to the immense effort expended here. Why, for example, would Le and Miller conclude (1999: 34) that "regional unemployment effects need further study" when decades" worth of ABS unemployment data have made it plain that regional and rural Australia have long supported the consistently highest aggregate levels of unemployment. Throughout 2000, for example, the big capital cities had an aggregate rate of unemployment around 7 percent; regional and rural Australia on the east coast, for example, had rates in excess of 10.5 percent. However, these observations become mere quibbles when set against their embarrassing, even alarming, self-admission that their risk index is not actually very good for anything.

We need to recall first the conclusion presented in their Synopsis—presumably the part of the report ministers and their advisers will find time to read—about the viability of their risk index. Quantifying the relationships between various factors and the incidence of unemployment, they have claimed, has practical policy implications. Le and Miller suggest, for example, that an inverse relationship between education and unemployment ought to mean that additional education is the way to reduce the probability of job success (1). Their findings, they argue, can also be used for case management. For example, if the research findings demonstrate that those who leave school early and who have poor English skills have high rates of unemployment, then those with such a combination of characteristics or other combinations known to be associated with high levels of unemployment should be case-managed (1). Quoting from the earlier work of Miller and Volker, Le and Miller argue that:

> Many of the groups distinguished under the risk index approach, therefore, are characterised by well-defined intervening factors. This implies that the risk index approach, and the associated study of unit-record data, have direct policy implications (2).

All of this, however, is subverted in the body of their report (see p. 39) when they explain that:

> ...the risk index is...a rather blunt instrument. It results in the categorisation *of individuals at risk of being unemployed who in fact spend 70% of the following year working*. Moreover it would also result in a pool of at risk persons in the population of approximately 700,000. *Such a pool does not appear to be an appropriate size on which to target policy* (emphasis ours).

If we wished to be bland, we would say that this is a surprising admission. It actually annuls the point of their report. To put it mildly, all the display of methodological sophistication and formal demonstrations notwithstanding, the central point of the exercise is entirely undone if it turns out that the risk index does not actually predict the behaviour they say it does. However, they claim that they have an escape hatch at hand when they suggest *they can preserve the value of constructing their risk index by focusing only on that part of the sample composing the 1—2 percent of "very high risk person""* or those with an "exceptionally high likelihood of being unemployed." Again, this claim merely compounds their problem. When it transpires that you can only use a tiny fragment of the population judged by the risk criteria to constitute the highest risk group as a basis for informing policy, program, or service delivery, then you really have to wonder about the value of the entire exercise.

Then there is the problem, which is not unique to this research, of the way the authors rely on a variety of rhetorical techniques, especially those of a mathematical kind. Presumably designed to persuade the reader, the mathematical and statistical techniques on display are in many cases actually all too likely to confuse an averagely intelligent, even well-read, reader.

From the outset, it is plain that the authors are out to construct a force field around their work which deploys the usual rhetorical devices open to econometricians, one that will deflect the ordinary intelligent reader from either understanding, let alone challenging, the assumptions or methods used. The rhetorical effect achieved in this kind of research is indeed on the surface formidable. All is smooth, calm, and confident yet largely unintelligible given the usual tests of inspection and literary accessibility deployed by the average intelligent reader. Even in the synopsis, this effect is at work when they (1999: ix) declare that:

> The categorisation of individuals...is undertaken using two types of risk index. The first of these uses all the estimated coefficients from the logit model to predict the risk of unemployment.

As is common among econometricians, there is a relentless use of mathematical presentation, which Le and Miller use to secure the authority and credibility of their claims and to persuade others. As Davis and Hersh (1987: 53) have noted:

> ..."mathematical certainty" is a byword for a level of certainty to which other subjects can only aspire...the level of advancement of a science has come to be judged by the extent to which it is mathematical.

As is the case in many other manifestations of this kind of formal presentation, it may also be pointless or misleading. Irrespective of the cleverness of the mathematical presentation, the fact is, as Le and Miller point out, their risk index is not a very good predictor of anything, given that most of the people surveyed who generate their risk index are working within a year. When in doubt, reach for a mathematical formula, drawing on the magic of numbers to impress readers with the objective analytic rigour and systematic quality of your claims. As Le and Miller explain, their model of unemployment can be expressed symbolically as:

$$U^*j = XjB = Ej \qquad \text{(equation A)}$$

In plain English, this translates as a claim that the risk of being unemployed is a result of all the alleged variables such as age or education level smoothed by taking into account the sampling error. Le and Miller say by way of "clarification":

> ...where U^*j is a latent variable that captures the propensity towards unemployment of individual j, X is a vector of observed factors (i.e., educational attainment, age, birthplace, etc.), B is a vector of coefficients to be estimated and E is a stochastic error term. In the first place the explanatory variables are restricted to those which have been used on a regular basis in previous research....This provides an appropriate basis for comparison across studies, hence the probability that a person will be unemployed is related to educational attainment (six dummy variables), age (quadratic function), sex (a dummy variable), marital status (three dummy variables), section of State (three dummy variables), birthplace...etc. (Le and Miller, 1999: 26−27).

This technique for securing their claims to knowledge continues unabated. The insistence on using these pseudo-scientific frameworks of authority, scientific terminology, and symbolic representation to convince their audience produces a convoluted and unnecessarily complex text that obfuscates, muddles, but hopefully impresses the reader. It includes a long list of terms and claims such as "binary indicators," "logit models," "algorithms," "probit models," "natural logarithms of the odds of the probability of unemployment (U) to the probability of employment (1−U)," "log (U)," "(1−U) is expressed as a linear combination of the explanatory variables" (27−28).

In terms of outlining the "logit model," Le and Miller explain that:

> Two outcomes are derived from U* with reference to an arbitrary threshold of zero. Thus, the individual is held to be unemployed (U=1) where U* exceeds zero, and is employed (U=0) otherwise (Le and Miller, 1999: 27).

We take it that means that you are either employed or you are unemployed, which in one sense is a logical banality. In another sense, it is nonsense. It implies a clear-cut distinction between "work" and "nonwork" to which a mathematical value can be given for purposes of making the equation work. Yet, it fails to cognise the actual complexity of the often dramatic experience many people with marginal attachment to the labour market— who may, for instance, have no skills, or very high-grade skills, have of working for short periods of time in full- or part-time work with intermittent unemployment. This simple binary logic also rather nicely ignores the problem of underemployment.

The authors of this style of mathematical presentation may feel they have established a satisfactory degree of expert distance between themselves and readers. However, the contradictory and illogical quality of the substantive research strategy and findings which characterises much of this research—and which is a feature that comes to the fore in Le and Miller (1999)—is so well camouflaged by the rhetoric of statistical presentation that it goes unchallenged, simply because too many readers have been put off from reading the text critically.

Davis and Hersh (1987: 57) have argued that four substantive considerations need to be kept in mind when reading and judging this kind of formal mathematical presentation.

- *Does the depth of the real-world problem justify the complexity of the mathematical model?*

We would say no, especially given that any or all attempts to locate the cause of modern unemployment in the deficits of a person ignore the more salient point that if there are no jobs available, the question of personal deficits or risk factors is simply irrelevant.

- *Are any genuine mathematical reasonings or nontrivial calculations carried out which require the resources of the mathematical model being proposed?*

Again, we say no. The equations being used are ill-fitting attempts to restate in a mystifying way the proposition, ready to be advanced in easy-to-read, plain English, which says that personal or social deficits are more important in explaining the unemployment of this or that person than the supply of jobs by employers and employing organisations.

- *Are the coefficients or parameters in the equations capable of being determined in a meaningful and reasonably accurate way?*

Again, we say no. A good case in point is the way the Le and Miller assign a numerical value to only two states: "unemployment" or "employment."

In the real world there are not simply two states and two numerical values as prescribed in this equation. There exists a whole spectrum of states of unemployment and employment in which time is of the essence. This refers both to (i) the extent to which someone is fully excluded from the labour market and for what length of time as well as to (ii) the gradations involved from being fully unemployed to the states of marginal employment. This goes to the question of how many hours of paid employment someone works set against their need or inclination to work longer hours but being unable to do so. The assumptions Le and Miller make pay no attention to these very real issues.

- *Are the conclusions capable of being tested against real-world data? Do any nonobvious practical conclusions follow from the analysis?*

In the first instance, the conclusions are capable of being tested, and on this occasion the claim that they have developed a viable index of risk is not warranted by the actual social behaviours of 70 percent of their sample.

A democratic culture depends on the capacity of producers/researchers and readers/consumers to converse, and conversation depends on a common language. Le and Miller have smothered some variously highly suspect techniques and "findings" in a dense and indigestible mathematical representation. They have not made a useful contribution to well-informed discussion about one of the most serious social problems of the past twenty-five years.

Even if the rhetoric of mathematics were of real scientific value in identifying risk factors for unemployment, another basic problem remains. The idea that it is sensible and useful to collect a lot of aggregate data about large numbers of people, then develop risk factors and search for those risk factors in real individual persons, is substantively an exercise in blighted logic.

One essential problem is how it is even possible to move from the collection and statistical analysis of large-scale data about the characteristics of populations to then identify the risk factors at the individual level to ascribe to real people. It is neither wise, nor is it possible, to use data representing characteristics found at a collective group level to make claims about particular real persons who manifest the features found at the aggregate level. In order to believe that this is wise and useful, it is necessary to ignore the problem of the fallacy of composition. The folly of this procedure is apparent in the fact that many graduates with Ph.D.s—who are white, middle-class, who live in leafy suburbs, and who are in their late twenties (i.e., who possess all the markers denoting a very low risk of unemployment)—have been found every year since the mid-1990s in graduate survey data to be unaccountably unemployed, and furthermore, in considerable numbers. This data suggests that graduates from some discipline areas such as the natural sciences actually sustain quite high levels of unemployment for some time after acquiring a tertiary qualification. While anecdotally it seems clear that many graduates when they do get a job end up working in industries or jobs with little, if any, relationship to their area of training, this is never treated as disconfirming human capital theory.

On the other hand, the assumption that unemployment is an individual experience and problem that is best identified in terms of individual risk factors—and not something arising, for example, from the supply of certain jobs—are embedded in Le and Miller"s report. There are major problems present in any exercise in methodological individualism, as in this project. The clear role played by the methodological and ontological assumptions associated with individualism (Arblaster 1989) and which are central to liberal economic theory—including, most notably, neoclassical models—is in evidence here.

The constitutive and metaphorical assumption operating here is that unemployment is a consequence of what occurs when individuals bearing a range of skills or human capital, and other attributes such as age or good looks or accident of birth (as with the country one is born in), enter as jobseekers into labour markets which they anticipate make them attractive to employers or not. Missing from this research is a consideration of the role of decisions and judgements made by employers and corporate entities (or firms) about their need for labour as a determinant of how many jobs will be made available to job seekers in a given period of time.

Le and Mller apply all this methodological prancing to an exercise almost perversely designed to miss the point. That point was made decades ago by C. Wright Mills when he observed that if in a city of 100,000 people one person was unemployed, that was a "personal tragedy," but if in that same city 10,000 people were unemployed that that was a "social problem." There is something odd about pursuing a research project designed to establish what role the personal qualities or attributes of a person play in producing a major social structural problem in a society with substantial long-term persistent unemployment affecting in 2001 on a quite unrealistic-cum-conservative estimate 7 percent of the work-age population. Such a commonsense understanding, however, must not be allowed to impede the march of social scientific research. In regard to the technical basis of this exercise, our concern is not about the intrinsic merits or demerits of the scientific technology and methodology being relied upon *per se*. Our concern is about the use/misuse of a technology which in a given problem context may well be useful, but on this occasion is not.

Conclusion

Paid employment has traditionally played an important role in giving young people a place within their communities as financially autonomous adults. Paid work provided not only an income and a relative economic autonomy, but also assisted in ushering "the adolescent" into "the adult world." Waged work provided an inner stability; as Beck explains: "the occupation...guarantees fundamental social experiences" (Beck 1997: 140). Paid employment, however, is in many cases no longer likely to be as available to young people. Beck (1997: 140) argues that paid employment will provide a basic form or means of security that it is said to have provided in the past:

> Just like the family...the occupation has lost many of its former assurances and protective functions. Along with their occupations, people lose an inner backbone of life that originated in the industrial epoch....Even outside of work, industrial society is a wage labor society through and through...in its joys and sorrows, in its concept of achievement, in its justification of inequality, in its social welfare laws, in its balance of power and in its politics and culture.

A significant part of the problem of "youth at risk," and more generally the youth problem since the mid-1970s, has been framed in terms of the absence of that reliable means of integration. The reality is, however, that it is highly unlikely that we will see a return to the kind of "full (male) employment" that we enjoyed after 1945. The full-time youth labour market will not reappear, nor under current conditions are we likely to see a return to full adult employment. It is likely that we will continue to see a shift to reinvent old forms of domestic service as a "filler" activity for young people who are full-time students, offering low-paid, menial work to the young workers.

Despite the disjunction taking place, and whatever we may think about the worth of the "work ethic," many young people still want a full-time job and consider this very important to them. As Foucault observed, the priority given to waged work and the morality of work is much more about virtue than it is about the need for sustenance. Historically, waged work has been important to young people for many reasons. As Wilson and Wyn show, employment meant:

> ...the opportunity to demonstrate competence and make a contribution; not simply for an employment or training opportunity..., but to meet people and develop friendships (Wilson and Wyn 1987: 12).

This returns us to the point Beck made in relation to work and its role in providing those fundamental experiences. Perhaps we need to think harder about: how, given the disappearance of full-time waged labour, can we provide those opportunities and "fundamental experiences" for young people?

Perhaps part of the solution in terms of livelihood is to separate income from labour. There is a clear role for major changes in income security policy involving the introduction of a Basic Income Scheme (van Parijs 1993; Frankel 1987; Tomlinson 1998). The more difficult question is, how do we provide experiences that present opportunities for young people regarding citizenship, for full involvement in important social experiences and relationships, to be effective, autonomous, and competent in our social, political, and economic worlds? On what basis are young people going to develop "future pathways" in relation to developing social and other relationships previously provided at sites of wage labour? Constraint, moral concern, and increased governance, mobilised through categories such as "youth at risk," and policies directed toward retaining all or most under-twenty-five year-olds in education, provide a lasting basis for hope.

Notes

[1] This explains the inability of welfare economics to produce explanations of why income inequality exists since there is no theory of income inequality apart from differential pricing of resources and goods (Hollander 1987: 93–97).

[2] The survey collected information on Job seekers, Labour Market Programme Participants, and a Population Reference Group for three years—1995, 1996, and 1997. Analysis for the "Risk Index" used the Population Reference Group, which consists of a random sample of the population, and the first two data sets (1995 and 1996).

Chapter Three: Risk and Homelessness: An Empirical Problem?

The methodological intemperance that characterises sociology and that spreads to the other "human sciences" stems...from this twofold contradictory movement: a deliberate and forceful distancing from any familiarity with what is real in order to achieve the distance and height of Science, and a no less deliberate and forceful effort to recover that familiarity.
(Pierre Manent, 1998: 55)

In this chapter we explore some of the ways the elements of a "science of risk" are developed around the theme of youth homelessness. Youth homelessness first became an important, even a high-profile, issue for public discussion and debate in the late 1980s. UNICEF in 1989 estimated that globally there may be as many as 100 million children and young people who were homeless. Brian Burdekin"s report on the situation in Australia in the late 1980s likewise put the problem firmly onto the local public agenda.

In Australia, like many other Western countries, we have seen the development and implementation of projects directed toward identifying those at risk (and even those "potentially at risk") of homelessness (Neil and Fopp 1992; Hagan and McCarthy 1997; Cordray and Pion 1997; Chamberlain and MacKenzie 1998). The primary purpose of such projects is to provide a basis for effective intervention by policy makers, governments, and the community sector, or what we call "government."

In the emerging "science of risk," there are particular styles of cognition which "discover" problems in particular ways. Here, we focus on the issues set loose by claims that both measuring the extent of youth homelessness and the risk factors involved are essentially "empirical problems" best addressed by the use of conventional social science research techniques. In Australia one research project (Chamberlain and MacKenzie 1998) offers a useful basis for assessing the value of the "empirical research practice" that underpins most risk research. We will analyse this in conjunction with a Canadian study of homeless young people in Toronto and Vancouver (Hagan and McCarthy 1997; Bessant 2001). In effect, we want to show how research into homelessness reveals how the problem, in this case of homelessness, comes to *be constituted through particular styles of reasoning*. As Dean and Hindess (1998: 9) note:

> Problems become known through grids of evaluation and judgement about objects that are far from self-evident. The study of government thus entails the study of modes of reasoning.

We argue that there are good reasons not to accept the proposition that the "empirical" research said to characterise the identification of homelessness or the risk factors involved is credible because it ostensibly reports in an "objective" fashion what is actually there.

Homeless Young People

From the start, in each project we are invited into the authoritative and verifiable world of the modern social sciences. Chamberlain and MacKenzie"s first sentence informs us that: "This book is the result of a research journey which has taken eight years" (1998: vii). Based on a survey that elicited responses from 99 percent of secondary schools, Chamberlain and MacKenzie (1998: ix) implemented a survey of 42,000 young people to identify those "at risk" of becoming homeless so as "to identify policies and practices that enable early intervention" to prevent youth homelessness. The assured voice of modern social science is present in their conclusion that:

> On the basis of these findings, it is possible to make generalisations about the "at risk" population in most communities. In a typical city school with 1000 students there will probably be about 100 to 140 young people (10 to 14 percent) who are possibly at risk at any point in time, and this will include 40 to 60 students (four to six percent) who are seriously at risk. The latter group are likely to be experiencing major problems in family relations. Most will not be happy at home, many will feel unsafe, and some will be running away (1998: 98).

Evident also is a scattering of tables throughout the Chamberlain and MacKenzie book, conveying a considerable amount of numerical information. Thus, the reader is assured that the product of this research will provide a credible basis for identifying "youth at risk." The reader"s confidence is justified because both projects rely on legitimate social scientific methods, that is, empirical surveys of young people "at risk" of homelessness.

Chamberlain and MacKenzie: Problems of Objectivity and the "Magic Kiss"

When social scientists acknowledge there is considerable controversy about the meaning of a concept, we cannot and should not expect this problem will be solved by an empirical exercise such as describing or measuring something that exists (e.g., the number of marbles in a bag). Social experiences such as poverty, homelessness, and unemployment do not have the kind of objective existence that, for example, might characterise a bag of marbles or a room full of chairs. Instead, these kinds of social issues depend on social definitions about which there may be little or no consensus. For example, it is not much good saying that unemployment is defined when people do not have a job. This would include a vast number of people, beginning with babies, children, and young people. Lacking a simple objective status also implies that it is no easy matter to go around counting the numbers of people said to be unemployed or homeless. Accepting this seems to jar the confidence of some social scientists, creating an uncertainty about aspects of their research program, and Chamberlain and MacKenzie (1998) appear to be no exception to this unease.

The critical retreat for social scientists who adhere to "the principle" of objectivity is the proposition that the scientific method in some way authorises all the claims made by scientists. The "scientific method" legitimises certain styles of understanding above others. It depends on measurement, replicability, and experimental procedures designed to isolate causal relationships, and the generation of explanatory, predictive statements are recognised as the hallmarks of the "scientific method." In terms of "scientific practice," principles such as naturalism, objectivism, and operationalism operate as authorised directives for good research practice. Danziger calls this framework the "Sleeping Beauty" model (1990: 2).

According to this model, the objects that science operates with or seeks to "know" already exist, and only await the magic awakening kiss of the scientific researcher to animate them and bring them into the province of Knowledge. Durkheim"s account of the nature of social scientific research is a good example of Danziger"s point. Durkheim (Giddens 1995: 352), defending the "thing-like" status of "social facts," says:

> What it demands is that the sociologist put himself in the same state of mind as the physicists, chemists or physiologists when they enquire into a hitherto unexplored region of the scientific domain. When he penetrates the social world, he must be aware that he is penetrating the unknown.

Practitioners of this model believe that the "social facts" already exist even if they have to be uncovered. Because social facts are orderly and actual entities means they can be measured, tested, and described accurately, then subjected to experimental (repeatable) procedures, for the purpose of establishing invariant relationships of causality and/or probability. However, for entities that do not have these qualities (such as "at riskness"), the processes of operationalising them mean that as abstract entities or as non-tangible phenomena they can nonetheless be rendered amenable to measurement, testing, description, or experiment for the purpose of establishing relations of covariance/invariance, etc.

This may explain why Chamberlain and MacKenzie operate with such a high level of conceptual confusion. This is revealed early when they acknowledge (1998: 16–21) seriatim that:

- There are many different definitions of "homelessness."
- Some writers have argued there are no correct definitions and that the concept is arbitrary, not very helpful, and/or should be abandoned.
- Certain definitions of homelessness which depend on the "perceptions" of young people constitute an "extreme form of relativism."
- This "relativism" can

> ...be overcome *theoretically* once it is recognized that "homelessness" and "inadequate housing" are socially constructed, cultural concepts that only make sense in a particular community at a given historical period...it is a cultural construct, but this does not mean that "homelessness" is just a matter of opinion, or that all definitions are "arbitrary" (1998: 19) (our emphasis).

Chamberlain and MacKenzie are eager to drape themselves in the security of objectivity. Yet, confronted with considerable differences about what "homelessness" or what "adequate housing" might mean, they resolve the puzzle in a "classic" way. Chamberlain and MacKenzie maintain that an "objective" "community standard" exists which reflects the standards of a particular culture or society regarding "homelessness." Thus, they claim that

> ...community standards are usually embedded in the housing practices of a society. These identify the conventions and cultural expectations of a community in an objective sense (1998: 19).

This assumption enables the social scientist to empirically gather data to demonstrate what "objectively" that homelessness is, and this is achieved by identifying anything which falls below "the standard." This is actually highly problematic because it depends on claims about the existence of a common, but not particularly useful, idea such as:

1. The notion a consensus exists in a "society" based on "shared community standards" "according to [which] the conventions and expectations of a particular culture" can be specified about what in this case constitutes "adequate housing" or "homelessness" (Chamberlain and MacKenzie 1998).
2. This claim depends on a prejudice shared by many sociologists about the concept of a consensual and singular "social system" called "society" or "culture."

This prejudice flies in the face of the problem that societies such as ours are marked by extreme inequalities in the distribution of economic resources such as income and wealth, or capital, producing a very wide distribution in people"s capacity to consume goods and services or to sustain their lifestyles. This is to say nothing about the no-less-marked array of culturally grounded variations in social and economic aspiration. Thus, any claim that there is either a convening or a consensus about something such as "adequate housing" is inherently problematic. Chamberlain and MacKenzie do not try to construct an index of homelessness; they simply (1998: 20) assert that there is a "benchmark" or a "minimum community standard," an assertion that is not actually demonstrated.

For social scientists such as Chamberlain and MacKenzie, their faith in the potency of "research methodology" offers some protection from any danger to which the dreaded vapours of "conceptual relativism" might expose them. Central to that faith in social science research methodology which comprises the "natural attitude" are core assumptions such as phenomenalism (i.e., that the concepts, entities, or objects that a discipline seeks to "know" are actually there); this is the Durkeimian (Giddens 1995: 351) postulate that "social facts" must have a "thingness" to them, without which they cannot become an object of scientific knowledge. (By this Durkheim means that they should have no "mental component".) "Social things" must also be amenable to measurement and the phenomena should display an innate orderliness and predicability.

The "natural attitude" entertained by empiricists (and positivists) maintains that "Reality" or "Nature" is simply there awaiting "the magic kiss" of the scientist-as-Prince-Charming (Danziger 1990). We say that all of the sciences work with constructive schemes which mandate and regulate certain assumptions and practices about what is to count as "real" and about what practices will produce credible knowledge. Though empiricists hate to admit it, this also means that there is a range of "scientific practices" which are set up to overcome the problem that some things do not exist in any way that makes a problem amenable to empirical study.

Operationalising the Category or Model

These assumptions underpin the commitment to practices such as operationalisation, representation, measurement, and repetition of those practices found in much social scientific research. Whatever social scientists who are committed to the "natural attitude" say about these practices, they are ultimately discursive and social in nature:

> The sentences in textbooks, the tables and figures in research reports, the patterned activities in research laboratories are first of all products of human construction whatever else they may be as well (Danziger 1990: 2).

Operationalism involves using a category for which there is no actual empirical referent (such as "homelessness" or "at riskness"). It involves establishing criteria that allow the research process to develop and define the phenomenon to be "discovered" and then "measured." As Chamberlain and MacKenzie (1998) explain, the category of "at risk" helps to grasp the otherwise elusive concept of "at risk." The reader also learns that any "at-risk" index needs to be identified numerically "because it is necessary to make a quantitative assessment of the at risk population" (1998: 89).

Evident here is the enactment of a standard inconsistency by empiricist researchers who are concerned with "objectivity" and the need to demonstrate that their work is "empirical."

This is despite the reality that the category of "at risk" is not empirical. Yet, this seems to be a relatively minor problem given that records, tables, indexes, and a variety of measurement processes are there to convince the laity otherwise. How did they do this? They explain:

> Our task was to design a survey to be filled out by secondary students in a classroom situation, which could identify young people who might be at risk. In order to do this it was necessary to operationalize the concept of "at risk" in a simple way, and to develop questions that would be easily comprehensible to students from Years 7 to 12 (1998: 91).

Perhaps it can be said in Chamberlain and MacKenzie"s favour that unlike their North American counterparts, they did at least demonstrate an awareness of the need, according to their own intellectual framework, to articulate the categories they were examining. Then again, Chamberlain and MacKenzie needed to do this because their research is so much more abstracted than the work of Hagan and McCarthy, who were actually spending time with, and talking to, the young people they were trying to find out about.

All this raises the question about how such researchers establish the "risk factors" and thus the substance of the questions? Chamberlain and MacKenzie do not say how explicitly, but it seems they used the "judgments" of certain welfare teachers at schools about what they saw as risk factors. They refer to this when explaining that "our operational definition of "at risk" is grounded in "the first order experience of these workers"" (1998: 90). These "judgments" are said to be far better than the "perceptions" of the young people they criticise as being so "relativistic."

Most of these "risk factors" allegedly related to "the family situation." Using the "risk factors" identified and with access to "a complex body of qualitative information," and using the fact that many months, if not years, of data collection and analysis have been invested in Chamberlain and MacKenzie"s project, the social scientists are well situated to construct a survey instrument using five questions scored from zero (no risk) to two (at risk) which asked questions such as "Have you run away from home in the past twelve months?" or "Do you feel safe at home?" (Chamberlain and MacKenzie 1998).

Even if the most simple criteria are used, namely that there has been an attempt to articulate what the links are between the alleged "at-risk" factors "known to be associated with health related [or social] condition[s] considered important to prevent," Chamberlain and MacKenzie (1998) have not been successful. They do not establish any links that could support their claim that they identified a population of "at-risk" young people.

It is worth noting that Chamberlain and MacKenzie appear to be offering a kind of risk assessment based on epidemiological research.[1] Typically, epidemiological research attempts to identify the "risk factors" for a wide range of social or health problems as well as uncovering any underlying etiology of lifestyle illnesses or epidemic infections. Rigorous epidemiological research involves establishing that:

> ...an aspect of personal behaviour or lifestyle, an environmental exposure, or an inborn or inherited characteristic...on the basis of epidemiological evidence is known to be associated with health related [or social] condition[s] considered important to prevent (Last 1988: 115—16).

Unfortunately, the research performed by Chamberlain and MacKenzie does not attempt to meet, let alone pass, this test. They have tried to advance the proposition that they can use aggregate data about large numbers of people and then apply that data or any findings from it to a particular person, arguing that the individual is "at risk." This is a completely unwarranted procedure. The reasoning used in this exercise involves taking from the epidemiological research which may show certain average values or deviations from the norm (based on investigations of large numbers of individual cases) and then turning to an actual single individual and saying to that person

"Because you exhibit factors A, B, and C, you are at risk of X." Such an assessment means moving from measures of central tendency such as averages to particular cases. As Gould argues, it relies on a peculiar jump in logic. As a statistician, Gould reminds us that

> ...reality is composed of varying individuals in populations and that variation itself is irreducible (1996: 3).

As Gould explains, "Central tendency is an abstraction, variation on the reality" (1996: 48–49). In other words, moving from a claim that X is true of the whole group to the claim that X is also true for each single member of the group cannot be done. Yet, even these useful preliminary warnings do not fully prepare us for what Chamberlain and MacKenzie offer (1998). For Chamberlain and MacKenzie, the risk factors are to be made known by asking questions such as "...whether the young person has...run away from home in the past twelve months?" (1998: 91). (Running away, they argue, is "usually a sign of serious problems at home"). The researchers simply assert that:

> In most cases where a young person is at risk there is a serious problem in family relations (1998: 91).

This statement is made without any justification or evidence, nor is there an indication given about whether or not those young people who reported these circumstances did actually leave home. What any of this actually refers to, or why it should be regarded as convincing, is not made clear. They have, in one act of omission, ignored the central requirement involved (Last 1988: 115–16): Identifying a "risk factor" involves establishing that some aspect of personal behaviour or lifestyle or environmental exposure, or an inborn or inherited characteristic, which on the basis of epidemiological evidence can be associated with health-related [or social] conditions, in fact exists.

The next step in securing objectivity (i.e., measurement) is to assign a particular risk factor a numerical weight so that the overall degree of "at riskness" can be "accurately determined." As Chamberlain and MacKenzie explain:

> A young person who had run away scored two, and those who had not scored zero. The second question asked...whether they felt "safe at

home". Everyone who did not feel safe scored two (Chamberlain and MacKenzie 1998: 91).

Other questions to be asked include whether they "get into a lot of conflict" with parents and would they like to move out soon, or whether they "feel happy at home" or not.

Scores are kept from zero, one or two depending on the answer (Chamberlain and MacKenzie, 1998: 91). "Taken together" (the reader is told), "these five questions provide an indicator of current family circumstances" and thus the level of risk of homelessness the young person faces (Chamberlain and MacKenzie, 1998: 91).

In their analysis, Chamberlain and MacKenzie subdivided the youth cohort into country regions, major regional city areas, middle class, traditional working class, and a "new working class" (located in the corridor outskirts of the city), Non-English-Speaking Background families, Anglo-Australians, and Australian Aboriginals (1998: 92—97). This means the proportion of those most at risk can be developed and the risk factors of children from specific backgrounds more readily identified by reference to their ethnic or socioeconomic status. If, for example, you are seen as belonging to the "new" or "traditional" working class, then you are measured as being at a far higher risk of being homeless than a young person from a "middle class" background (1998: 95).

Not only are there problems with many of the assumptions underlying the questions asked, but there are also difficulties with the assumptions underlying the categories used. For categories such as "middle class" or "traditional working class" to be operationalized assumes the existence of actually homogenous groups whose experiences can be isolated from other groups /classes and whose members actually do share characteristics. Inherent in such categories is an assumption about the existence of a homogeneity, or general essence or trait shared by all members of the specified group. While it is true that many groups of people share some specific experiences, there is a question whether we can extend those quite specific commonalities to talk about a "middle class" or "traditional working class" or "rural" young people.

Hagan and McCarthy on Canadian Homeless Youth

In Canada in the late 1980s, two researchers, John Hagan and Bill McCarthy (1997), initiated a research program taking the lives and experiences of young homeless people in Toronto and Vancouver as their principal focus. Hagan and McCarthy are primarily interested in developing a "criminological research project" that takes seriously the experiences of young people who are homeless. There are many salutary differences between their work and that of Chamberlain and MacKenzie—and some worrying similarities.

Hagan and McCarthy argue that "street youth are not a significant focus for contemporary criminology." They are interested in "peering" into the "black box" of street crime to point to possible "indicators of criminal opportunities" and promisingly they say they want to document the experiences of the young people. In this one regard, Hagan and McCarthy mark an important move beyond the tired and largely irrelevant work of researchers who work on captive research targets in schools to construct their index of "at riskness" about youth issues. (This remark applies to Chamberlain and MacKenzie"s work in which they use "self-reports" from young people somewhat, and the reports of experts in the schooling system much more, to tell us about the risk of homelessness.) Hagan and McCarthy"s book is an argument for returning to the street-scene and for renewing attention to its implications for understanding crime (Hagan and McCarthy 1997: 21). This at least seems to be heading in the right direction.

The best parts of the book are those parts where they step back and let the young people speak for themselves. This act of self-denial on the part of an academic cohort long wedded to social ventriloquism is very hard for social scientists to practice—though the wisdom of less-talking-and-more-listening has recently received the imprimatur of no less a sociologist than Pierre Bourdieu (Bourdieu et al. 1999: 607—27).[2] Even so, Hagan and McCarthy (1997: 24) insist on weaving their own categories ("incompatibility with family and stepfamily members, disrupted and dysfunctional families, neglectful parents, coercive and abusive parents, parental rejection...") into the vivid stories told by the young people "contained in the respondents" own descriptions of their experiences".

Yet, there are worrying signs aplenty, evident especially in Hagan and McCarthy"s proposal to drop a complex web of "scientific" statistical and comparative analyses over that experience so as to draw out the "causal variable" that can enable them to better identify the "social forces," both "ontogenetic" and "sociogenic," that impel the young people onto the streets. The possibility that the young people"s stories say plainly that they found themselves in a given situation and chose what seemed to them the best or only course of action is far less scientific a finding than Hagan and McCarthy"s complex references to "bivariate coefficients." It is not for nothing that in the foreword to their book, Short observes that theirs is an "all-too-rare combination of rigorous theoretical and empirical enquiry applied to a significant research problem." Decoded, Short means to say that the book offers a thick paste of criminological and sociological myths ("rigorous theoretical inquiry") heavily reliant on an endless stream of metaphors presented and operationalised as if the metaphors actually denominate the thick textures of reality ("rigorous empirical inquiry").

As Hagan and McCarthy (1997: 4) indicate in that complacent way modern social scientists have about them, "attention to sampling, measurement and sophisticated multivariate analysis has increasingly dominated criminological research." Such variables, they argue, have a sizeable and direct effect on all types of criminal activity and will therefore enable them to "intervene between our foreground measure of situational adversity (i.e., nights on the streets) and crime" (Hagan and McCarthy 1997: 135). What they are actually doing is setting loose a powerful and unresolved tension between the research which we think makes their work genuinely valuable (i.e., the insights into lived experience) and the flight from the empirical where they posit measurement technologies (represented, for example, by relentless operationalising and measurement of variables and categories) which constitute their kind of empirical research. Equally, the highfalutin talk about using theoretical constructs such as social class or theoretical models such as control and strain theories, represents no gain in terms of assisting us to pay attention to people"s lives, but offers these social scientists another excuse to flee those people"s lives and the actual social setting in which homelessness becomes a part of contemporary social experience.

Hagan and McCarthy (1997: 11) engage in the usual exercises in conceptual clarification that mark out the abstracted nature of much social scientific research which is based on the practice of operationalisation. They note that the term "youth" applies to people "roughly between the ages of fifteen and twenty-four" (1998: 11). On homelessness, the usual equivocations are present but they are ruthlessly suppressed. Noting that there are differences between young people who are "on" the streets (i.e., who work on the streets but who return at night or on weekends to their family) and those who are "of" the streets (i.e., who have no family to return to), Hagan and McCarthy decide to banish any reference to the reasons why young people are not living at home and they adopt the simple and inclusive criterion "does not have a permanent address" as the mark of the homeless young person.

To say that they are dependent on an utterly conventional account of "crime" is hardly sufficient to distinguish them from the thousands of other conventional criminologists. So once again we are invited to take a "walk on the wild side" and observe and "tut-tut" at "the low life" as they engage in minor and serious theft, assault, prostitution, and drug use. As Hagan and McCarthy observe (mustering an awful lot of moral seriousness):

> We find that 46 percent of the homeless respondents made drug sales, 49 percent stole goods valued up to $50 and 27 percent broke into homes and businesses.

Ultimately, however, they cannot resist the urge to measure and compare, and the result is a profligacy of categories, operationalised and measured, in which their own social prejudices—largely unacknowledged by the researchers as such—comingle with the lived experiences of the young people. Given that Hagan and McCarthy are interested in young people already on the street to determine the likelihood of them engaging in criminal activities, we see a different set of indicators emerge (i.e., employment status of parent, whether the family is "intact," "erratic parenting," "explosive parenting," school involvement, and involvement in theft) (63–64).

They use a class matrix derived from Erik Olin Wright"s (1985) class model, comprising the "surplus population" (identified by an unemployed head of family), workers, petty-bourgeois, managers, and employers. There are several unhappy features about their class model.

First, they find no trouble in agreeing with Wright (1985: 137) when he writes that:

> All things being equal, all units within a given class should be more like each other than like units in other classes *with respect to whatever it is that class is meant to explain.*

This prime piece of gobbledygook entirely blanks out any recognition (found, for example, in the work of E. P. Thompson) that class is a relational category in which real people produce and reproduce real social practices in figurations. Instead, their model licences a kind of determinist heuristic which first constructs then "explains" categories such as "crime," "delinquency," or "antisocial behaviours" as if these were objective behavioural correlates which just are. There is no reflexive understanding of how these categories are produced as categories by particular agents or their social practices in a given class setting. That is, there is, again, no reflexive treatment of the categories being used and manipulated—an act of extraordinary amnesia given the tradition of social critique associated with the symbolic interactionist tradition about the production of social categories involved in statistical enumeration as with Cicourel (1968).

Second, and undeterred by any of these considerations, Hagan and McCarthy march boldly on to announce their commitment to the measurement of class categories, and the correlation of class, with their own model of strain and control theories:

> For example we categorise a family in which one parent is a supervisor and the other a worker, as belonging to the supervisor class regardless of the gender of the person working as a supervisor.

Why this should be a useful way of approaching class, let alone why they embrace the conceit involved in "measuring" "class," is never explained: Presumably, this is all too self-evident to warrant any explication.

We do not doubt that "class," which as a category has almost disappeared from the modern social sciences, is an important idea when deployed in ways that recognise the principles of interconnection and the effects of a radically unequal distribution of economic, political, and intellectual resources and the reliance on practical and symbolic violence involved in maintaining a class order. That is, there is a strong case for developing a fully social account of class as a relational category which requires researchers to pay attention to the interrelations between economic, political, and intellectual practices and the distribution of access to these resources.

This is not what Hagan and McCarthy offer. For them, "class" is a category deployed so as to replicate, once more, what William Ryan (1975) indicted as the strategy of "blaming the victim." "Class" for Hagan and McCarthy is about the idea that some classes, especially the surplus population, produce antisocial behaviours, beginning with bad parenting that then generates "ontogenetically" and "sociogenetically" youth homelessness and then crime.

Like so much of this dismal tradition, they offer a simple set of identities between poverty, belonging to the "surplus population," and the antisocial dispositions that membership in that class group seems to entail. Hagan and McCarthy"s use of the category "surplus population" is profoundly shaming to social science and needs to be apologised for: We need to recollect the use made in other societies of categories such as "life unworthy of living" or "the asocials" to feel that there is any evidence of ethical sensitivity or social responsibility in their use of language. For Hagan and McCarthy, class positions exist only to be correlated with measures for an "intact family," understood in terms of two biological parents, and a range of measures designed to establish the presence of factors such as "erratic parenting," "explosive violence," and "levels of school involvement and commitment."

This leads to what for them is the inescapable conclusion that "harsh class background experiences cause crime…that youth from surplus populations are more likely to take to the streets and that the experience of street life itself increases serious theft" (1997: 77).

What again the particular discursive techniques and practices of empiricist social science reproduce in their work is a "black box" explanation typically found in what used to be called the "culture of class/poverty" tradition. Like other and earlier exponents of that tradition, Hagan and McCarthy offer up explanations couched in terms of the deficiencies and deficits of the families and class groups from which the homeless young people are drawn. All of the problems which are used to "explain" why some young people become homeless are located in the specific and deficient patterns of class, family, and schooling life.

In effect, as when Hagan and McCarthy (1997: 56) suggest that "parental economic problems can lead to the mistreatment of children and youths" we rely on them finding a "positive association between parental unemployment and parental violence to children," so also when they suggest that "poverty increases the risk of harsh inconsistent punishment" or that "family income loss and instability are linked to neglectful and volatile parenting" we are invited to contemplate the "otherness" of the surplus population and their engrained antisocial tendencies.

Hagan and McCarthy are simply unable to satisfactorily locate these experiences in a fully and comprehensively developed account of a social setting in which, for example, the acts of commission and omission on the part of governments, police forces, the mass media, welfare agencies, schools, or corporations play any role in producing the social experience of homelessness. If, with Richard Rorty, we stop asking "Is it true?" (as a prelude to one more attempt to secure some epistemic certainty by methodological means) and ask "What is it good for?" then the answer has to be: "Not much." Ultimately, like so many social scienctists of this ilk, Hagan and McCarthy are more interested in showing off their command of the whizzbangery of their "explanatory variables" and their undoubted skill at deploying "logistics" and "probit estimates" (1997: 91–101) to an audience of other social scientists than in offering the wider community insight and understanding to what is undoubtedly a major social problem.

Conclusion

In the nineteenth century Thomas Carlyle referred to economics as the "dismal science." Without doubting the continuing salience of that animadversion, we would add that in the twentieth century "empirical sociology" can make a late bid to be included in that characterisation. The Polish writer Tadeusz Borowski once suggested that the prime task facing him was to "develop a language capable of expressing human experience in verifiable language." The preoccupation with "scientific methodology," as we have tried to show here, does not necessarily deliver that capacity. As Lepenies (1988) has shown, there has long been a debate within the social sciences between the claims of a hermeneutic and literary tradition and the claims of a science of society which sought to ape the proper sciences of nature. The application of those scientific methods in regard to the determination of "at riskness" has licensed a profligate, unreflective, and careless proliferation of social research categories which do not aid insight nor aid the practical determination of policies capable of generating anything more than "bright ideas," when what is needed are "good ideas."

Notes

[1] Different types of research operate within the epidemiological research program. They include:
   1. "case studies" researching people who have a particular problem;
   2. "correlation studies," which survey the entire population for correlations between factors a, b, and c and the problem;
   3. "cross-sectional surveys," which sample a complete population; or
   4. a "cohort study," which selects a part of a population by age or ethnicity, etc.

[2] As Bourdieu (Bourdieu et al. 1999: 608) puts it:

The positivist dream of an epistemological state of perfect innocence papers over the fact that the crucial difference is not between a science that effects a construction and one that does not, but between a science that does this without knowing it and one that, being aware of the work of construction, strives to discover and master as completely as possible the nature of its inevitable acts of construction, and the equally inevitable effects those acts produce…

…in the interview process…we have done everything in our power to control the effects of the symbolic violence exerted through that relationship. We have tried to set up a relationship of active and methodical listening, as far removed from the pure laissez-faire of the non-directive interview as from the interventionism of the questionnaire.

Chapter Four: Crime and the Science of Risk

Have you read any criminology texts? They are staggering. And I say this out of astonishment, not aggressiveness, because I fail to comprehend how the discourse of criminology has been able to go on at this level. One has the impression that it is of such utility,...for the working of the system that it does not even need to seek a theoretical justification for itself.
(*Michel Foucault, 1980: 47—48*)

Contemporary debates about crime have been informed by the idea that liberal-democratic societies are now confronted either by the "fact" of significant levels of "crime" or an increasing "crime rate" (Garland 1996). The so-called "crime problem" is said to be pervasive, all-consuming, and a grave risk to all Australians (Hogg and Brown 1998). We argue that there is little evidence to justify the popular anxiety about crime and the idea that we confront an "epidemic of crime" or a crime rate that is "out of control." The fact that there is little evidence to justify such anxiety has had little if any effect on governments in Australia: Governments have found it convenient to "get tough" on crime by introducing a range of punitive "law and order" measures such as mandatory sentencing.

Juvenile crime has come in for particular attention, with many state and territory governments in Australia promoting draconian policies that too often breach international conventions on human rights (Sidoti 1998). Governments also talk about getting tough on the "causes of crime," leading to the introduction of visible and repressive forms of governance in the shape of punitive laws and highly visible forms of crime prevention. It is in such a setting that risk has become a central category in much of our contemporary social science research and in policy making.

In this chapter we look at the first of two case studies, the first Australian, the second, British (which is discussed in chapter 5), to analyse how the idea of risk has been used in criminological studies about crime and its likely causes and strategies for prevention.

The Australian Experience

Most Australian criminologists (and those working in cognate disciplines such as sociology and psychology) who research "delinquency" or juvenile crime believe they are doing "empirical research." Much of this research is designed to shed light on why some young people do "it," and is done in the hope that it might assist governments, police, or welfare agencies to develop possible responses to, or even "prevent," the problem. Our view is that most of this "empirical" research does not actually engage with young people and the kinds of "action" and "experience" which constitute the activity being scrutinised. Rather, much of this research either seeks (i) to generate "objective" data as a preliminary to generating the analysis of covariance or else (ii) to analyse or otherwise manipulate the data produced by state police agencies or the Australian Bureau of Statistics. In either case, the operating assumptions underpinning these research interventions are, as we have been arguing, the work of a conventional model of social science.

Conventional criminologists, psychologists, and sociologists assume inter alia that (a) "crime" and the "crime rate" are objective and stable "social facts" and that (b), actors are constrained to act in ways which structural variables such as socioeconomic status, education level, subcultural contexts, biological factors or family status impel them to do. In effect, as Pierre Manent (1998: 54) indicates, all such attempts to "know" reality are underwritten by the "sociological viewpoint" which they rely on and which:

> ...adopts the viewpoint of the spectator. The viewpoint of the spectator is all the more pure and scientific in that it accords no real initiative whatever to the agent or agents, but considers their actions or their works as the necessary effect of necessary causes.

We think it would be better if social researchers paid more attention to a social phenomenology of "action," feeling, and "experience" (Katz 1988) situated in real figurations (Elias 1987) which could provide the core conceptual and "empirical" focus for a reconstituted and revived sociological enterprise.

As Flyvbjerg (2000) argues, such a reconstituted social science would be less preoccupied with aping the physical sciences, or be fussed about securing its epistemological guarantees of truth or objectivity, and be more preoccupied with recognising and developing the capacity for "practical judgment." However, our intention here is not to mount an argument about how to do this or why it would be worth doing. Rather, we want here to show in what ways the emerging science of risk sits within the contemporary government project. Investigations of the government project call for

- the study of problematisations
- analysis of the social or institutional site of the problematisation process
- analysis of particular styles of reasoning

We do this by focusing on three recent exemplary research reports:

- the Queensland Criminal Justice Commission report *Youth, Crime and Justice in Queensland* (Queensland Criminal Justice Commission 1992)
- the Commonwealth Government"s National Crime Prevention project (1999) report, *Pathways to Prevention*
- the Juvenile Justice Program (1999) of the Queensland Department of Family, Youth and Children Issues Paper, *Causes and Juvenile Delinquency*

The Study of Problematisations: The Crime Problem

If we begin with the *study of problematisations*, we should ask how the qualities of the problem are being identified and established, and what is said about the attributes of those who are being governed?

In 1992 the Queensland Criminal Justice Commission (1992) released a report, *Youth, Crime and Justice in Queensland*.[1] The Criminal Justice Commission report (1992) is about the "practical-administrative" aspects of crime control. That is, it is concerned with developing specific programs to deal with the "small section of the population" who are "disproportionately represented in the criminal population" (O"Connor 1992: 63). The knowledge gained through the research is designed to support a "targeted approach" to work with offenders and their families. With the data in hand, the task for policy makers and practitioners is then to draw on that material when planning systems of intervention that address the specific "needs" of those under the formal supervision of governmental agencies.

In terms of characterising their own approach to the "crime problem," the Criminal Justice Commission identifies the risk category with a politically "progressive" approach to crime control. They identify as "progressive" such things as the development of crime prevention programs and the pursuit of community alternatives to custody which are seen as offering a less-harmful approach to juvenile justice than more punitive and retributive approaches.

As to the nature of the problem they are addressing, the Criminal Justice Commission notes that there are numerous competing explanations of juvenile crime and that theories of juvenile crime deriving from such epistemological anchors have tended to inform policy and practice in the administration of juvenile justice over recent decades (Queensland Criminal Justice Commission 1992: 49—53). In seeking ways of dealing with juvenile crime, the authors of the report cite the work of Potas, Vining, and Wilson (1990), who outline a range of programs specifically designed for "at-risk" offenders. It also cites the French government"s (now defunct) Bonnemaison crime prevention program and other initiatives in the areas of preschool and employment training (for instance, the Perry preschool and the "Job Corps" programs) as "non-coercive and integrated" approaches to crime management (O"Connor 1992: 55). Such projects, although apparently "successful" in reducing crime rates (albeit for limited periods and under certain conditions), are nonetheless discussed in terms of their usefulness as prevention projects for at-risk young people. In other words, it is the control of crime and the preservation of social order that takes precedence over all other matters.

Along the way the Criminal Justice Commission (1992) ignores several well-understood problems. They slide over the socially constructed nature of the "crime problem." The "crime problem" is discussed as if official government statistics provide an unequivocally objective "picture" of the problem. The Criminal Justice Commission also assumes that the "population" in question is discrete, readily identifiable, and suitable for appropriate state intervention, even though the report fails to identify which population it has in mind.

At the centre of such considerations are taken-for-granted categories of crime and criminality. The crimes of the urban poor have always been defined as more consistent and a more serious threat to social order than, for example, the crimes of state or corporate officials. "Street crime" is regarded as more visible, immediate, and potent in terms of undermining social order. The very definition of what constitutes "crime" continues to reflect the disparities, ambiguities, and relativistic nature of such conceptions in the liberal state. (This applies particularly in the arena of corporate crime where breaches of the law are dealt with by civil courts or commissions of inquiry rather than in the criminal courts.) The problematic nature of such statistics regarding the construction of the "juvenile crime problem" is glossed over. Inevitably, this avoids questions relating to the way in which systems of crime control are assembled to manage crimes of the urban and rural poor (Hudson 1996, Carrington 1993, Bessant 1998). It overlooks, too, evidence of the pervasive nature of crime across all sections of the population. In this way the report adds weight to the technicist approach to juvenile crime control in which calculations of risk are seen as central to the design of preventive programs in supposedly "crime-prone" neighbourhoods and communities.

With such matters in mind, the phenomenologist Alfred Schutz (1986) launched (in 1940) a critique of the "nihilism of modernism." In asking where social researchers got their categories from, Schutz posed a central question about the politics of discourse of which most empiricists appear unable to answer or even to recognise the point.

Constituting the Crime Problem

After seven years not much has changed. In March 1999, the Commonwealth Government"s National Crime Prevention (1999) project team released its report, *Pathways to Prevention*. Again, the central organising concept in the document is "risk," identified in a host of individual, familial, community, and social factors.[2]

Again, in characterising the nature of the problem ("juvenile crime") and their approach to it, the authors of the report embrace a progressive crime prevention framework informed by an "enlightened social scientific" research project committed to social inclusion and citizenship (National Crime Prevention 1999: 5).

Equally firmly, they reject what they call a conservative "law and order" diagnosis based on "single-cause" explanations such as bad genes or dysfunctional parenting. They also reject simple punitive responses such as increased police powers and mandatory sentencing.

The report is grounded in the very modern and popular discourse of risk. Accordingly, they argue that:

> ...the roots of criminal offending are complex and cumulative...embedded in social as well as personal histories. To uncover significant risk factors that are the facilitating conditions for entry into a criminal career requires a life course perspective that views each young offender as someone who is developing over the life course and in specific social settings.

On this basis, the report (1999: 5) develops a case for "crime control" strategies based on the promise to reveal

> ...scientifically persuasive evidence...that interventions early in life can have long term impacts on crime and other social problems such as substance abuse.[3]

In constructing the problem of juvenile "crime," the authors of the 1999 report, like their many predecessors, take for granted the fundamental categories such as "crime" and "youth."

Crime has long been constituted by conventional criminologists largely as conduct associated with "the poor" the "urban working class" and/or "young people." All that remains for the criminologist is to record, catalogue, classify, and report on the nature and extent of the "crime problem" (Garland 1997). This approach to the study of crime characterised not only the individualistic focus of neoclassical criminology at the end of the nineteenth century but also the early sociological forays into "street corner" crime and delinquency associated with the Chicago school of the 1920s (Taylor, Walton, and Young 1973: 91–138). In the late 1990s when the "crime problem" is thought about, and when official statistics are drawn on to inform accounts of "increasing crime," the idea of crime is associated with the "traditional" offences of the urban poor: robbery, theft, burglary, assault, drunkenness, and so forth along with more modern crimes such as drug abuse (Garland 1996).

The 1999 report struggles ineffectually against this conventional bias. On the one hand, it argues that the conservative law "n" order tradition is

> ... exclusionary, presupposing a core of "decent people" distinct from a criminal element that must be contained if it cannot be excluded.

This is a problem because as "progressives" they know that the

> ...developmental perspective is inclusive, embedding potential young offenders in their families and embedding their families in the wider society (National Crime Prevention 1999: 5).

Yet this insight is quickly forgotten. The report soon makes it plain that the kinds of crime, and the kind of population in which they are interested, are in essence the crimes of the urban poor. In coded language for the "underclass," the report makes it clear which population should be the targets of intervention. This is evident when it is noted for example, that

> ...a number of conditions...strongly related to juvenile participation in crime, poverty, sole parent families and crowded dwellings—taken together—account for 56% of the variance...in a path analysis, poverty, sole parent families and crowded dwellings emerge as influencing juvenile participation in crime (National Crime Prevention 1999: 40).

The population under study is thus identified in terms of criminogenic ("at-risk") lifestyles. State officials direct their attention toward this population, irrespective of whether such intervention is desired or warranted or not. No effort is made in the report to theorise the connection between policing (in its broadest sense) and criminalisation, or to examine the discursive practices that have led to such an intense scrutiny of those living in poverty in urban areas. Rather, a technical approach to risk management is proposed to fix the crime problem as identified by the report. Questions of governmental mismanagement and the failure of "social responsibility" in catering to the ravages of the restructuring process or the failure of governments to invest in social and physical infrastructure are glossed over entirely. Instead, the state directs its disciplinary gaze at the most powerless sections of our society under the pretext of "crime prevention."

The Formation and Shaping of Identity

The study of modes of government also attempts to *identify the formation and shaping of the identities, capacities, and statuses of members of the population,* in this case of young people. In the new science of risk, identifying the problem represented by young people begins by pointing to the number of "at-risk" types of young person (QDFYC 1999: 1).

The foundational assumptions of modernist criminology are writ large in the way the pathways to "delinquency" and "criminality" are identified by the authors of the *Pathways to Prevention* report. In a fashion long rendered "normal" by modernist social science survey-based research, as well as by questionnaires carried in popular magazines, the paper identifies different "types" of "offender":

- the "non-offender"
- the "child who falls in with the wrong crowd"
- the "mischief child"
- the "mild offender" (i.e., at risk)
- the "serious offender"

The "non-offender" has few if any law-breaking friends, participates far more in and enjoys school activities, is well disposed to the police and law, has a mild temper, and is optimistic about the future. The non-offender is also "materially advantaged" and "likely to have a positive attitude to upholding conventional norms."

The "mild offender" is "at risk" of becoming a "serious offender." This "type" of young person is one who falls in with the "wrong crowd" or is simply a "mischief child." He/she has some of the characteristics of the serious offender, although in a less developed and hardened form. The "mischief child" operates more independently and spontaneously than other young people and is likely to engage in "foolish and impulsive...and rarely repeated" nuisance behaviours. He/she has a high level of concentration, is prone to thrill seeking, gets angry easily, and is occasionally "uncontrollable" (QDFYC 1999: 3—5). The "thrill-seeking" and "high-temper" characteristics of potential offenders are apparently reinforced by loyal associations with law-breaking friends and "negative attitudes to the police and law" (QDFYC 1999: 3).

Finally, there is the "serious offender." The identikit of this "type" is constructed in terms of personal characteristics such as

- a disposition to "thrill seeking" and "high temper"
- "nonparticipation in conventional school activities"
- lack of adherence to "conventional norms"
- difficulties in or reluctance to participate in "conventional activities"

The "serious offender," for example, is described as likely to "have friends who break the law." He or she has "a negative attitude to the police and the law," enjoys "thrill seeking," "finds it hard to trust and depend on others, tends to worry about people getting to know them too well, believes that they should not bother people with their problems," has a "short temper," is pessimistic about the future, is "materially disadvantaged," and has already been in contact with the juvenile justice system.

There are at least two fundamental problems with this account of the identities of the young people being characterised in terms of "types."

There is the sweeping nature of the typologies which suggests an inability to appreciate the genuine complexity of human experience. The very attempt to slot the answers given by the research subject"s responses into preconceived categories works against any in-depth understanding of the dimensions of lived experience. It is doubtful whether a self-administered (and excessively long and intrusive) questionnaire such as that used in the Sibling Study can draw out the complex meanings and experiences of young people. This mitigates against any appreciation of the attitudes and values on the part of real young people, let alone the basis of their attitudes, for example to the police.

Is it possible, if one probes a little deeper, that most young people entertain complex sets of ideas about the police, and that many young people might support police intervention in some instances and oppose it in others? It is also likely that some young people"s experiences of the police—perhaps as a result of being "moved on," harassed or abused, or treated unfairly by them—may have some bearing on the way police officers are perceived by some young people (White 1994b). This is different from the stark alternatives set up by the "attitudes" inventory in the Sibling Study where the choice is between a "positive" or a "negative" view of police. Identifying attitudes (e.g., to police, parents, school) is given the weight it has presumably because of the assumption that the attitude leads directly to an action; this is a most imprudent assumption. Worse, much of this kind of research denies young people any capacity for agency. Rather, they become "cultural dopes" constrained to act in limited ways both by their own "psychological" dispositions and/or by certain "social structural factors" that have to do with gender, ethnicity, socioeconomic background, and so forth.

Moreover, this kind of research neither identifies nor defends its assumption that the clustering of attributes according to certain "types" of offenders depends on

- the claim that each member of the assumed group actually shares a uniform set of "tendencies" and
- that the population falls neatly into such a set of subgroups.

Is the differentiation between the "normal" child as against the inherently "antisocial," "serious," and "at-risk" offender anything more than a grotesque exercise in stereotyping? In short, the typologies articulated here are crude caricatures more reminiscent of "popular" stereotypes found in pop psychology than the complex result of considered empirical research. One of the early "empirical" researchers, Alfred Kinsey, reminded his readers in the 1940s that his research into sexual behaviour confirmed his sense that nature abhorred pigeonholes.

The mapping of risk factors in the context of strictly "developmental" concerns tends to avoid the deep and penetrating questions associated with policing in late capitalist economies and neoliberal states. As is well known, such policing is typified by its "differential" nature. That is, some individuals and groups come in for more police attention than others. "The urban poor," young people, "working-class families," people on public housing estates, and Aboriginal communities are the major targets of state-sponsored intervention (Carrington 1993). The strategic targeting of these "problem populations" for purposes of crime prevention is reflective more of the processes of governance in late modernity than of any simple attempt to do away with "social problems." This point is ignored in the problem-fixing approach of the *Pathways to Prevention* report. What constitutes crime and how the forces of law and order are marshalled to deal with the "crime problem" are rendered irrelevant to the imperatives of technical analysis and problem fixing.

This central conceptual failure is covered up in a welter of technical and sophisticated deliberations about the measurement of risk factors. The identification of risk factors as a means of informing various early intervention programs reflects a technical approach to the question of crime control, "technical" in the sense that the *primary* intention is to provide policy makers and program managers with the raw material (data, risk factors, etc.) to pursue their ameliorative and interventionist ambitions. Questions about what "crime," "criminality," and "crime prevention" might mean in the political and discursive contexts of our time are avoided. What remains is an "empirical" endeavour dedicated to the task of eradicating an undertheorised, unclear, but seemingly major "threat to social order."

By constantly avoiding such issues, the *Pathways* report secures a renewed emphasis on identifying the risk factors—such as genetic dispositions, family "disorganisation," drug and alcohol use, or sexual promiscuity—that turn some families and individuals into "criminal." These crimes are associated most closely with the "underclass," or "criminal subcultures." Indeed, it is worth noting that the subjects researched in the *Pathways* report consist primarily of the urban poor, indigenous people, single mothers, and the unemployed—the very people who have been constituted as part of an "underclass." This reveals the preoccupations in many criminological quarters.

With the new millennium it seems that the criminological gaze has returned once more with a vengeance to the crimes of the urban poor and the young. Rarely is crime equated in the criminological imagination with companies that engage in systematic and deadly pollution, with illegal corporate criminal activity, or with the crimes of the state and its officials. It is as though the cloak of respectability—readily claimed by the elites who manage the corporate world—and the state apparatus have been successfully applied to deflect the sustained critical attentions of criminologists and others. The value of investigating "criminal subcultures" among senior businessmen, political elites, or leading financiers rarely seems to occur to modern criminologists. (When it does it is usually because there is evidence of so compelling a kind that not even criminologists can avoid it.) In this way the normal tendencies of criminology work to maintain an utterly conventional view of the kind of governance that is socially legitimate remain, and, are therefore deeply misguided.

One important effect of this should be noted. In the drive toward risk-based and customised interventions proposed by the *Pathways to Prevention* report, there is a tendency to render invisible those who are subject to intervention. The voices of children, young people, and their families—their lived experiences, lived realities, motives, and meanings—are buried under the deadweight of statistical data and multifactorial analysis. The taken-for-granted character of the "crime problem" compounds the hackneyed and presumptuous view that crime is only what the working class, the young, poor people, and members of the "underclass" do. Yet, no effort is made phenomenologically (or in any other way) to generate insight into or to understand the point of view of those caught in the shifts, changes, and realignments of social change. Rather, those who are "at risk" are transformed into docile, even silent, subjects distinguished only by their potential for disorder.

Styles of Reasoning

As we have noted, the study of government does not assume that problems exist in themselves, but rather that they *must be constituted through particular styles of reasoning*. What this means can be established when we look closely at the rhetoric invoked in the evolution of a science of risk.

We have suggested that modern criminology is a tension-filled field of study, teaching, and research, caught between an ambitious "science of causes" epitomised by John Braithwaite"s (1989) continued espousal of the value of searching for a "general theory of crime" and a more pragmatic, policy-oriented administrative project seeking to use science in the service of management and control. This synthesis is exemplified in another Queensland-based social scientific research project, referred to, until its demise, as "the Sibling Study."

In 1992, when discussing future directions for juvenile justice in Queensland, the Criminal Justice Commission report calls for "a longitudinal study of juveniles to *identify factors associated with participation in and desistance from crime*; recidivism studies; and evaluation of crime prevention programs" (Queensland Criminal Justice Commission 1992: 63) (our emphasis). Why such research is required given the already-existing large quantity of longitudinal research (albeit often highly inconclusive) found in numerous international research projects (Farrington 1994; West 1982) is not made clear.

The success of such longitudinal studies is said to require the collection of substantial and ongoing bio-psycho-social and demographic information on each young person included in that research. One way such a project could be undertaken is to collect information through schools, health authorities, and other government departments on a sample of young people. To ensure the confidentiality of the data, it is argued that such research should be undertaken by a body independent of criminal justice agencies and the state (O"Connor 1992: 64). The point is reiterated that

> ...in the medium and long term, longitudinal research offers the most powerful strategy in identifying factors associated with participation in and desistance from crime (1992: 63).

What all this means is suggested in the architecture of the "Sibling Study."[4]

The Sibling Study project aimed to uncover the "psycho-social and ecological determinants of delinquent behaviour." The scientific part of the project was exemplified in the intention to analyse hundreds of variables from a sample of 1,125 young people aged twelve to eighteen years. This sample was drawn from various "cohorts" of young people in school, under the supervision of the "Family Services Department," and in "the community" (i.e., on "the street," in "the community," and/or through "personal contact"), taking account of mixed sibling pairs (spanning no more than three years" difference in age) from diverse "advantaged" and "disadvantaged" backgrounds. The governmental aspect of the project is suggested when the study"s project manager notes that all of this science is designed to "provide a plethora of data regarding young people, their experience of family life, school and the justice system, their attitudes and behaviour" (Kennedy 1997: 2).

A second observation about the risk research project in terms of *the problematisation process* is the way it depends on a relatively narrow band of insights and assumptions found among developmental psychologists.

This is suggested, for example, in the way the Commonwealth Government"s 1999 *Pathways to Prevention* report focused on a quite narrow band of "crime prevention" program options which were heavily reliant on research informed by the "developmental" perspective.[5] This psychopathological emphasis is, for example, clearly revealed in an extensive, yet highly "selective," bibliography.[6]

The absences in this literature review are as striking as is the privileging of developmental psychology. Significantly, there was very little sociological literature in the review, which is surprising given the nature of the project and the presence of two sociologists on the team. Entirely absent is any critical social theory. Just as striking is the wholesale omission of any historical texts dealing with questions of crime and crime control, or any of those important contributions by the likes of Stan Cohen and others who (especially during the 1970s and 1980s) drew attention to the major epistemological shortcomings of the types of research favoured by the *Pathways* report. The literature review in the report is not simply "selective," it is breathtaking in its avoidance of any reference to a body of work that has contested the very foundations of developmental research. These absences play their part in the substantive report which offers a truncated and partial understanding of "crime" and its "causes."

The research design of the Sibling Study likewise relies on numerous epistemological and methodological assumptions about what constitutes a proper research design representing best social scientific practice.[7] In spite of persistent criticism of the epistemic and ontological prejudices and assumptions upon which the "scientific method" rests, they are presented without any defence or justification. These assumptions include the "need" to employ repeatable forms of data collection and rely on methods that facilitate "objective" measurement.

The project uses a plethora of psychometric research instruments drawn from a diverse range of attitudinal, behavioural, and self-assessment rating scales. These include:

- the Delinquency Disposition Scale
- the Parental Bonding Instrument
- the Rigby Attitude to Authority Scale
- the Attitude to Self and Others Scale
- the Impulsivity and Monotony Avoidance Scale
- the Sensation Seeking Scale
- the Sex Role Attitudes Scale
- Body Image Scales
- the Australian Self-Report Delinquency Scale

The mere listing of these scientific instruments alone may convince most readers that this is authentically scientific research indeed. As noted in an appendix to the study code book, the sources of these scales are largely psychological, biological, and medical texts. The Parental Bonding Instrument, for example, is drawn from an article in the *British Journal of Medical Psychology*, while the Impulsivity and Monotony Avoidance Scale is drawn from an edited text titled *Biological Bases of Sensation Seeking, Impulsivity and Anxiety*. By grounding their approach in a paradigm that emphasises psycho-medical and biological explanations, the researchers of the study lay the foundation for a body of authoritative empirical knowledge. As is typical of modernist social science and its preference for treating social data as "observables" amenable to objective study, the study also offers no reflexive critique of these scales.[8] The study actually draws on a vocabulary of images and categories about "adolescents" and "delinquency" which social science experts and researchers have developed throughout the twentieth century. The study inherits the legacy of an extensive criminological sociobiological tradition in which subjects are empirically measured and surveyed in an effort to "discover" the factors which predispose them to crime.

The detail of the research questionnaire serves to reassure anyone anxious about the objectivity or scientific precision of the project that they need not worry. The data linked to the scales is derived from a self-administered questionnaire of staggering proportions. In a code book which summarises the interim results of responses to over four hundred questions, each response is divided according to value, frequency, percent, valid percent, and cumulative percent. The questions cover almost every conceivable facet of an individual"s being: from their family, household, and neighbourhood characteristics to the degree and kind of parental supervision and discipline, affection, and cohesion, to school and employment situation, moral development, body image, and even sexual experiences.[9] The research also manifests an interest in biological matters. The young person, for example, is asked: "How tall are you without shoes?" "How much do you weigh without clothes and shoes?" "How satisfied are you with the following things about your body? (your present weight, the shape of your body, your clothes size, your general appearance?)".

Why would these researchers be concerned about a young person"s physical features (such as their height or weight), and what is the relevance of information about the young person"s perceptions of their body? How are these factors related to identifying the causes of offensive behaviour? Are short people more likely to be criminal, or are short people who are dissatisfied with their small stature more at risk than tall people or those who are happy with their body? The significance of these and other similar questions is not articulated clearly in terms their perceived relations to "crime" or "delinquency." Indeed, the study is reminiscent of a lot of the research conducted during the immediate post-1945 period in Britain and America when social and economic variables sat uncomfortably alongside a range of oblique psychological and biological factors.

These scales are designed to capture what are said to be individual dispositions such as a person"s values, their psychological or emotional functioning, or actual behaviours. These are invariably measured against some "norm" where the confusion between the statistical meaning of this is invariably confused with its moral meaning. One of the key forms of abstraction in the emergent biopolitics of population management initiated in the late nineteenth century has been a kind of statistics which defines the characteristics of the population against a statistical norm. It means that what we come to see as a norm is an artifact of a methodology or technique; a curve on a graph which quickly becomes widely incorporated into our beliefs about what is normal or what is risky behaviour, incorporating such things as adolescent development, behaviour, and educational attainment. Variation on what is defined as the norm becomes an aberration requiring treatment.

There is a general failure in the Sibling Study to acknowledge the well-known cross-cultural difficulties associated with individualised scales of measurement (Rose, Lewontin, and

Kamin 1987: 31). This problem becomes particularly acute in a multicultural society such as Australia in which attempts to measure characteristics along uniform scales make little or no practical or cultural sense. The study"s preference for privileging these individualistic rating scales also indicates a worrying absence of a properly conceived sensitivity to sociological considerations, which is somewhat surprising since a sociologist is one of the project directors. Indeed, the scales may serve to gloss over the complex questions associated with cultural diversity and may generate concerns similar to those aroused over the now much-discredited Intelligence Quotient (IQ) scales. While the use of these scales may be serving a rhetorical function, that is, they embody the authority of properly objective quantitative data and methodologies, they may do little, however, to further our understanding of the complex processes associated with juvenile crime in Australia.

Risk Factors

Like the Sibling Study, the "risk factors" identified by the authors of the *Pathways to Prevention* study (National Crime Prevention 1999: 11) are derived from numerous longitudinal studies and include "genetic and biological characteristics of the child, family characteristics of the child, family characteristics, stressful life events and community or cultural factors." They are also heavily yet silently dependent on long-standing views about the essential nature of adolescence.

Much of the at-risk literature depends on "popular" and "social scientific" discourses about adolescence as a period in the lifecycle that is inherently agonistic and concerned with making a transition from childhood to adulthood, which is itself said to be a risk-ridden project. As Kelly (1998: 33) notes, discourses of youth-at-risk mobilise a form of probabilistic thinking about certain preferred or ideal Adult futures, and the present behaviours of young people. For Kelly, this kind of calculative reasoning attempts to construct statistically valid, causal relationships between these different configurations (33).

Yet, contrary to common sense and the twentieth-century literature on lifecycles, as Christine Griffin (1993) points out, there is no biological basis for the ways in which the categories "childhood," "adolescence," and "youth" have been either constituted or understood. Since the work of Phillipe Aries, it has been increasingly accepted that the idea of the lifecycle needs to be represented as an historical and cultural artifact.[10] Within the lifecycle idea can be found so-called phases of the lifecycle such as "childhood" and "adulthood," which also possess their own discrete history which locates its relationship to specific social actors and institutions. There is a history around the constitution of a discourse about "childhood" which would examine the period from the late seventeenth into the twentieth century and an equivalent history of "adolescence" which would focus largely on the twentieth century; the publication of G. Stanley Hall"s book on adolescence in 1904 is a conventional beginning point (Griffin 1993). In both histories we would note the "double hermeneutic" at work as "prescription" increasingly merges with "description."

In their table of risk and protective factors, the authors identify a long list of psycho-bio-medical antecedents under the heading "Child Factors." These include: prematurity, low birth weight, disability, low intelligence, difficult temperament, insecure attachment, poor social skills, lack of empathy, hyperactivity / disruptive, and impulsivity. Under "Family Factors," "Life Events," and "Community and Cultural Factors," there are an assortment of indicators reflecting the multiplicity of risk indicators. Along with aspects of family form, structure, and functioning, the authors refer to significant events associated with family life (such as separation, divorce, and bereavement) and the nature of school experience ("deviant peer group," "poor attachment to school," inadequate behaviour management, etc). Under "Community and Cultural Factors," the authors cite a number of structural considerations (socioeconomic disadvantage, neighbourhood violence and crime, etc.) and cultural matters such as male portrayals of violence and other cultural forms of violent expression.

The long-standing commitment to empirico-positivist techniques of research (for example, covariance) sits easily in the background of this report on other research. Drawing on longitudinal studies, the authors acknowledge that risk factors cannot be easily clustered for predictive purposes because they "tend to co-occur and be interrelated," "operate cumulatively," and are combined and interactive (National Crime Prevention 1999: 15). It is therefore not possible to calibrate a precise mix or cluster of variables that lead to crime. Rather, any predispositional state relates to the developmental stage and particular set of cumulative circumstances surrounding the individual. Thus, according to the authors: "the critical factors may be the total number and the spacing of cumulative risk factors" (National Crime Prevention 1999: 30). Given the extraordinary set of causal factors identified in the report, it would, of course, be foolhardy to suggest the possibility of an accurate forecasting of criminal behaviour. Yet, this poses a problem for the researchers in that the very rationale of a "pathways" project is that causative signposts can and should be identified.

A way out of this impasse, according to the report, is "to package risk and protective factors in terms of their impact on a smaller set of underlying processes or mediators" (National Crime Prevention 1999: 15). The explanatory package, therefore, may thus include reference to delayed "social maturity" of an individual, "modelling" of deviant lifestyles, and the "social reinforcement" of adult-centred activities (National Crime Prevention 1999: 16). Such mediating processes, say the authors, need to be seen in their periodic and dynamic contexts (even though these are never clearly articulated). Given the authors" own cautionary tone about identifying the particular range of factors that may (or may not) contribute to the onset of criminality, the careful reader may nonetheless be left with an overwhelming feeling of uncertainty about what constitutes the "causal analysis" the authors claim to be offering. There is a distinct sense here of "factorial overload" present in the listing of spectacular arrays of risk factors which, despite their location in vague "mediating" contexts, leave the observer in a state of transfixion.

The report spares no effort in seeking to reveal the vast number of factors that place some people "at risk." Yet, the very scale of the multiple and imbricated risk factors supposedly involved in offending is a weakness rather than a strength. The lists of at-risk factors, conceived in narrow developmental terms, are so wide ranging as to render any attempt at prediction extremely difficult, if not impossible—a point tacitly acknowledged by the report (1999: 138—39). The key lists (under the headings of "individual," and "community") are like giant nets which capture entire populations of children, young people, and their families, who may now be considered a potential risk to social order. They thus become targets for intervention, ripe for the disciplinary attentions of officials and experts.

Three Problems

There are three basic problems with this style of reasoning. The first is the simple problem that the persistent search for the predictive factors that "cause" crime either in a direct or a stochastic fashion has been largely fruitless. Katz (1988: 5) summarises this point:

> Whatever the validity of the hereditary, psychological, and social-ecological conditions of crime, many of those in the identified causal categories do not commit crime. Many people who do commit crime do not fit the causal categories. Many who do fit the background categories and later committed crime, go for long periods without committing or attempting to commit the crime to which the theory directs them.

This critique has not and will not stop the criminological industry in its pursuit of causal explanation. Notwithstanding the fact that some of the things the report calls for, such as better funding for public health and educational services, are desirable in themselves, little attempt is made to appreciate the broad, underlying forces that shape the "order of things" in the late modern state. The identification of "social problems" and ways of fixing them squares with liberal agendas that are concerned more with the maintenance of a certain kind of "social order" than with fundamental systemic change.

Moreover, the cataloguing of risk factors depends on a vast literature produced since the 1940s on delinquent and criminal children and adolescents, much of which is committed to identifying the emotional, psychological, cultural, and social deficits both of the offenders and their families. There appears to be a high degree of insensitivity to basic issues of class, gender, age, and ethnicity in the selection of populations for research, evident in the refusal of mainstream criminologists to systematically research the families and the lives of elite or middle-class white people, a framework which all too accurately mirrors the policing and regulatory activities directed against subaltern populations.

In a closely related fashion, there is a refusal in certain exercises in the way they overlook the researcher"s own moral and political values. The fact that their values are reinserted into the categories being measured, and that they are central to the research discourse, is ignored. As Caspi et al. (1995) point out, categories such as "inadequate parental supervision," "impulsivity," "sluggishness," or the all-consuming "at-risk" category, tend to reveal more about the ethnocentric and class-centric views and prejudices of the researchers than they do about the world to which they are applied.

Finally, the reductionism that underwrites most empiricist research has the effect of blanking out the actual social world in which the research is being done, a world which—minimally—includes both the researcher and the research population. Positivist researchers like to reduce their analyses to single or "cluster" explanations of complex social phenomena. Thus, in locating the onset of delinquency in the "family dynamics" of poor or working-class families, the researchers abstract such behaviour from its wider social and economic contexts, simultaneously seeming to ignore their own cultural norms while silently using them to locate deficiencies in the lives of the (subordinated) research populations. The frequent emphasis given to the "internal dynamics" of "the family" or the "community" (as in the case of the *Pathways* report) means that any of these larger social contexts are located in the vague hinterlands of the "environment." Thus, "factors" (even if related to "structural" conditions) become abstracted artifacts appropriate only for purposes of measurement rather than for any sort of reflexive or theoretical exercise.

Conclusion

In this chapter we investigated the "science of risk" and claims about its capacity to inform us about young people and the risks they present to themselves and others. To critically review the application of at-risk concepts to young people, two representative case studies are drawn on, with attention given to the ways they are informed by functionalist sociology. The discovery of the youth-at-risk category has largely supplanted older categories such as "delinquency" and "maladjustment" that were foundational to the sociology of deviance. Yet, the methodologies, epistemological assumptions, and politics of governance inherent in the older projects remain the same.

Too much risk-based research relies on normative assumptions about social and economic dependence of young people, which, when given expression and legitimacy through the research findings, reinforce the authority of discourses of "youth" as dependent. Much of the youth-at-risk research tends to make assumptions about the category of youth as dependent and in need of close supervision. Risk-based research authorises researchers as expert speakers about homeless youth at the same time as it delegitimates young people as speakers and active subjects capable of framing the problems in different ways.

Some sociologists may have wondered what has happened to the "sociology of deviance" which loomed large as one of mainstays of an older "mainstream sociology." Some sociologists (Sumner 1994) have even gone as far as to write an obituary for the sociology of deviance. Reports about the death of the "sociology of deviance" may, however, be premature. They should look no further than the "new" "science of risk."

The faith placed in the "scientific method," coupled with the failure to think through the connections between class, power, policing, and deviancy, is itself indicative of a philosophical and epistemological nihilism. This nihilism allows empiricists to claim they are simply researching the "observable" while actually sanctioning them to invent the categories (i.e., various types of risk) they can operationalise. One result is a proliferation of empirical categories which, so long as they pass the basic tests of operationalisability, replicability, etc., assume an ontological status—that is, these "abstract" categories then become "real" and "purposeful" for the purpose of producing objective knowledge.

These research practices result from a largely atheoretical approach to research where the primary business is apparently to "identify" and "predict" the particular range of factors that can be identified and correlated, in this case with delinquency. The *Pathways to Prevention* report makes no attempt to theorise its findings or to deal with awkward methodological issues such as the inherent "constitutive abstraction" involved in all social research. That is, there is a process where most social scientific research categories are taken from the life world of people, reworked by researchers and theorists before being taken back and imposed on the life world of ordinary people. Otherwise, they are invented by the researchers/theorists before being imposed on the life worlds of ordinary people.

The attempt to reduce risk to produce "pro-social" behaviour is, of course, hardly unique to the *Pathways* report. Indeed, risk reduction projects are now central to crime control agendas in the liberal state (Muncie 1999). We might take a standard example of research (Schweinhart, Barnes, and Weikart 1993) which "operationalised" "pro-social behaviour" in terms of nine key criteria, including:

- making and expressing choices, plans, and decisions
- solving problems and taking care of one"s own needs
- expressing feelings in words
- participating in group routines
- being sensitive to the needs, feelings, and interests of others
- building relationships with children and adults
- creating and experiencing collaborative effort
- dealing with social conflict

Given that much of empirical research concludes that "broken," poor, and "criminogenic" families do *not* exhibit these qualities (an absence which then becomes a *prima facie* basis for "explaining" their descent into crime), it would be an interesting exercise were a researcher to attempt to identify these "pro-social" characteristics in the life and work settings of elite, white males in business or politics, academia, or various professional settings. Indeed, it is worth asking repeatedly why so much persistent attention has been applied to particular sections of the population? Or why the disciplinary gaze has been so selective and tailored to the imperatives of crime prevention?

Notes

[1] It was written by Ian O'Connor from the Department of Social Work and Social Policy at the University of Queensland. Although the report refers to "risk" (the quotation marks perhaps suggesting some concern with the concept), there is no detailed critical analysis of the category nor is there any inquiry into the likely effects of its use in shaping intervention strategies.

[2] In focusing on the crime control risk discourse identified earlier, it is important to note that while the projects in question may appear distinct and separate (concentrating on particular sets of policy and practice applications, or on cross-institutional research into juvenile crime), they nonetheless constitute an ensemble of cross-institutional practices, procedures, reflections, calculations, and strategies that allow the exercise of specific forms of power. Each project is connected at numerous points, deriving their approach to the problem of juvenile crime from the same paradigmatic source; namely, positivism. The institutional connections and interdependence are evident in the language used, in the cross-fertilisation of ideas, and in the crossover of personnel associated with each project. For example, we find that the Criminal Justice Commission Report of 1992 had a direct bearing on the creation of "the Sibling Study" insofar as recommendations in the report were ultimately translated into a longitudinal research project. This in turn led to policy statements emanating from the QDFYC such as a discussion paper titled "Causes and Juvenile Delinquency" (1999). As we will show, the latter paper is significant in that it draws on the Sibling Study data to develop a typology of at-risk young people. Further, Ross Homel, perhaps the leading exponent of crime prevention in Australia, had a direct and important lead role in the *Pathways to Prevention* project, the Sibling Study, and the Queensland state government crime prevention policy. Two of his colleagues in the Sibling Study also figure in the team that produced the *Pathways to Prevention* report. These sorts of relationships suggest a close collaborative involvement in a range of important research and policy initiatives at both the state and national levels. Such collaboration is significant insofar as it suggests not simply a close cross-institutional working alliance between academics and others but also (and more importantly) a collective commitment to the production of certain bodies of knowledge (Sibley 1995). Indeed, the knowledge base in all the projects discussed has a clear epistemological direction: namely that derived from the individualism inherent in developmental psychology. The point here is that this "meeting of minds" (albeit from different disciplinary backgrounds) reflects the way in which bodies of knowledge are produced and reproduced through certain professional alliances and systems of institutional support. The "ascendancy" or "hegemony" of modes of thought are in part a reflection of this interweaving process where powerful figures (professors and senior policy makers) articulate bodies of knowledge that become the conventional wisdoms of the day. This is clearly the case in contemporary juvenile crime discourse where the notion of risk, evident in major governmental projects, is central to the policy and practice in this area. It is perhaps here that we see most incisively the means by which discourses legitimate particular disciplinary practices.

[3] According to Ross Homel, a contributor to the report and a noted advocate of "risk criminology," the entire "crime prevention" project hinges on the identification of those "at-risk" factors that predispose some juveniles (rather than others) to crime. For Homel, "early intervention" involves a "womb-to-classroom" process aimed at those sections of the "urban poor" who suffer most from a lack of "parenting skills" and family support, along with a range of other criminogenic "risk factors" (*The Australian*, 7 December 1998).

[4] While we are yet to see the final results of this mammoth study, some hint of what the Sibling Study will produce is contained in an Issues Paper prepared by the Juvenile Justice Program of the Department of Family, Youth and Children titled "Causes of Juvenile Delinquency" and based on data drawn from the Sibling Study.

[5] David Farrington, the Cambridge-based doyen of developmental and longitudinal research, is cited nineteen times alongside other luminaries in the field of delinquency research such as John McCord (who receives a mere five mentions). Articles by Farrington with titles such as "Early Developmental Prevention of Juvenile Delinquency" and "Early Predictors of Adolescent Aggression and Adult Violence," fit well into the explanatory frameworks adopted by the *Pathways to Prevention* report.

[6] A total of 210 references are noted, with the vast majority being drawn from psychologically oriented journals and books. The literature covers a range of developmental concerns ranging from early childhood development issues (from "aggression" to signs of "antisocial behaviour"), child abuse and neglect, life-course research, intervention outcomes (mainly in relation to therapeutic and family-based initiatives), substance abuse, and other forms of "conduct disorder."

[7] The Australian Research Council-funded Sibling Study project has the support of "industry partners," including the Queensland Criminal Justice Commission, the Queensland Department of Justice, and the Queensland Corrective Services Commission. Funded for three years, the Sibling Study replicates many of the previous longitudinal studies conducted by criminologists in England, Canada, New Zealand, and the United States (see Utting, Beight, and Hendrickson 1993; Farrington 1994).

[8] The possibility that a scale designed to "measure" for example, "antiauthority attitudes" has first to define the criteria that will constitute the category—in effect, inventing the phenomena to which the category can then be applied—is never entertained by modernist social scientists. There may be some use in doing this in regard to some categories such as "unemployment" but only so long as no one actually believes the numbers refer to anything "real." The political implications of believing that one can measure, and even define, antiauthority attitudes in a value-neutral way are far more worrying.

[9] In relation to the young people's sexual life, the researchers ask: "Some young people today sleep with other people, while other young people don't. What about you? Do you ever sleep with someone? Have you slept with someone in the last month? Why did you sleep with this person?" Why establish such a line of questioning? Is the assumption that those who do "sleep" with someone else are more likely to commit criminal behaviour?

[10] The obvious biological aspects of infancy or of adolescence cannot be denied. However, this does not allow us to ignore the primarily social and cultural means whereby these periods of life have been made symbolically meaningful. The ways in which elaborate discourses about how both of these phases, childhood and adolescence, have been developed over the past two centuries cannot be overlooked.

Chapter Five: Risk and Crime Control: The British Experience

In a time when politicians are unwilling to concentrate on robust social and economic intervention to counter social problems, and eager to demonstrate that they are equally "tough" on both crime and the "family," any policy which identifies poor child-rearing practices and weak parental control as the fundamental problem is a political godsend.
(Pitts, 2001: 15)

Like Australia and the United States, Britain has recently made the category of risk central to discourses underpinning the control and regulation of crime (Muncie 1999). This has been most graphically displayed in the attempted prevention and reduction of youth crime through the 1990s. Indeed, crime committed by young people has preoccupied politicians and social policy makers to the extent that this issue has become ostensibly one of the most alarming and pressing "social problems" currently facing England (Pitts and Hope 1998).

Not surprisingly, public concern over "youth crime" has led to the introduction of a raft of governmental "solutions" aimed largely at minimising the apparent threat posed by "the growing ranks" of "marginalised," "disaffected," and "excluded" young people. Inner-city "riots" and concerns over the emergence of "antisocial" behaviours have further heightened popular concerns over the perceived threat posed by certain sections of the youth population. There is now a well-entrenched belief—at least in some quarters—that youth crime is reaching "epidemic" proportions (Muncie 1999; Garland 2001). Numerous media accounts of troublesome and disruptive school pupils, "adolescent" drugtakers, "youth gangs," and stories of "teenage violence" have strengthened the many negative typifications associated with young people. "Fear of crime" surveys, inflammatory speeches by "get tough" politicians, pronouncements by media "shockjocks," and reports by campaigning news journalists have added to a prevailing public sense of "ontological insecurity" about youth crime in the United Kingdom (Young 1999).

And yet, as Muncie (1999: 249—50) points out, governmental responses in Britain and elsewhere to "problem youth" and "juvenile crime waves" have produced a range of competing and often contradictory discourses:

> Social policy for young people is generally constructed around three competing discourses: young people as *either* the producers of trouble for others *or* as vulnerable and in need of protection *or* as deficient and in need of supervision and training.

Such accounts often overlap and vary according to the particularities of public sentiment and governmental interest. Over recent years it has become increasingly apparent that a popular assumption exists that certain sections of the youth population require intervention if the threats and dangers they apparently pose are to be addressed effectively (Muncie 1999: 250).

As in other Western countries, a range of government programs and regulatory projects has characterised the response to "youth problems" in general and to youth crime in particular. "Targeting" those most "troublesome" or "vulnerable youth," such measures are directed toward regulating and controlling the behaviours of young people and to ensuring their compliance with various legal codes and moral strictures. A range of experts have overseen the implementation of programs, schemes, and various "community-based" initiatives.

In England as elsewhere, what distinguishes these new interventions from the "welfarism" of the 1960s and 1970s is the emphasis on the category of "risk." Nowhere has this concept been applied more systematically than in relation to young people regarded as a threat to the social order. As we have detailed in previous chapters, its elevation into operational categories (used to calibrate levels of potential criminality among specific youth populations) bears all the hallmarks of research methodologies which take their foundationalist cues from the natural sciences.

Though this is hardly a novelty peculiar to our own time, the transposition of this "forensic concept" from the natural sciences to human affairs signals a shift from humanist-liberal discourses associated with "welfarism" to the "techno-scientific" articulations of risk, promoted most avidly in the domain of crime control by academic psychologists. As Lupton (1999: 5) points out, this techno-scientific project involves the search for various "predispositional" risk factors across a wide range of areas ranging from health and housing to education and crime:

> The focus of research in these fields is the identification of risks, mapping their causal factors, building predictive models of risk relations and people"s responses to various types of risk and proposing ways of limiting the effects of risk. These inquires are undertaken adopting a rationalist approach which assumes that expert scientific measurement and calculation is the most appropriate standpoint from which to proceed. Such researchers may be described, therefore, as adopting a realist approach to risk.

In Britain, the introduction of techno-scientific accounts of "youth at risk of crime" into routine operational practices of youth crime prevention has occurred in a context informed increasingly by individualised approaches to criminal justice.

Blair"s "New Labour" government has apparently given its blessing to the ascendancy of risk-based crime prevention. This appears to be the only way to make sense of the introduction of the *Crime and Disorder Act 1998*. This legislative intervention was based on recommendations of the Youth Justice Task Force established by Prime Minister Tony Blair in 1997. The aims of the act included speeding up the processes of juvenile justice, encouraging a greater sense of awareness and responsibility among offenders, integrating the idea of reparation into the criminal justice system, and heightening parental responsibility. It was also hoped that government might better address youth problems associated with drug use and literacy. The category of risk proved pivotal to many of these measures, designed not only to streamline the processing of youth offenders through the criminal justice system, but also to set in train a new interdepartmental and centrally monitored approach to "targeted" intervention.

Given the dynamics set loose in the election campaign, the new Blair government was very keen to appear "tough" on law and order and to actively counter the ad hoc nature of intervention associated with the "welfarism" of earlier decades. As Pitts (2001: 16) argues:

> "Toughness" for New Labour may mean the extension of custodial confinement and the community supervision of a broader range of

young offenders and troublesome children, but its stated purpose is to provide a forum in which "evidence-based" programs can be administered in a setting bounded by administrative protections against violations of children"s rights."

Unlike the deterministic explanatory frameworks espoused under "welfarism," Blair"s reformed system of juvenile justice would, at least in its legislative form, be designed to focus largely on "toughening up" on youth crime by holding offenders directly responsible for their actions. Additionally, the act ushered in a range of measures designed to regulate the behaviours of young people, including longer sentences for certain categories of crime, more community supervision orders, curfews, and electronic tagging for those aged ten years and over. As Pitts observes (2001: 15), these measures represented a "repudiation" of earlier approaches to youth justice which sought to attribute offending to "social conditions," restrict involvement of offenders in the criminal justice system, and/or to keep them out of the system altogether. The New Labour government regarded these as

> ...soft options which failed to confront the moral dimension of youth crime and disregarded the "right" of victims. However, the strategy diverged from developments in the USA, in its unwillingness to adopt explicitly "cued" measures such as the "Boot Camps," "House of Pain" regimes and "Chain Gangs" which have reemerged in several US youth justice systems in recent time "(Pitts 2001: 16).

The impetus to create a coordinated juvenile justice system which was "tough but fair" gathered pace in the wake of the killing in 1993 of toddler James Bulger by two ten-year-old boys. Many commentators have argued that this event finally "dealt with the problem of the soft approach" said to have been associated with welfarism. Indeed, since the Bulger case,

> ...there has been a steady movement away from strategies of informalism and nominalisation and the abandonment of attempts to divert less serious young offenders from prosecution and custody....This has been accompanied by a steady growth of custodial disposals for 15—18 year olds, and the introduction of new types of secure and custodial penalties and institutions for youngsters aged between 12 and 14 (Pitts 2001: 20).

While the prevailing emphasis of New Labour"s approach to youth justice has been a reliance on tough new sentencing provisions, the government has also sought to address those factors which purportedly led some young people to offend. Indeed, it is in the domain of New Labour"s juvenile crime prevention policies that we see a very clear articulation of risk as an operational concept used to legitimate a range of interventionist policies and practices. Yet, the question of which factors or individuals and families were to be targeted rested squarely on the particular explanatory narratives which New Labour had at its disposal.

Laying the Epistemological Foundations: The Case of "Misspent Youth"

A number of official reports published between 1993 and 1997 provided much of the "knowledge base" underpinning New Labour"s approach to juvenile justice. What emerges from these reports is a consensus about the supposed "causes of crime." *Crime and the Family*, by New Labour policy advisers at the Social Policy Research Institute (Utting, Bright, and Hendrickson 1993), the Home Office"s consultative document, *Tackling the Causes of Crime* (1996), *Misspent Youth: Young People and Crime* by the Audit Commission (1999), and last, but certainly not least, New Labour"s White Paper, *No More Excuses* (1997), all pointed to the same conclusion: that youth crime could be attributed directly to what went on in the family. *Crime and the Family* spelled this assertion out in no uncertain terms: "the tangled roots of delinquency lie, to a considerable extent, inside the family."

Perhaps the most sophisticated articulation of the "root" causes of crime emerged in the Audit Commission"s report, *Misspent Youth*. The report, published in 1996, established the foundations on which New Labour was to launch its approach to youth crime prevention. The report echoed politicians" concerns about the "disproportionate" number of young people from "deprived areas" involved in (mainly property) crime and the cost (estimated at over 1 billion pounds) of dealing with this problem. It also highlighted a range of other "antisocial" behaviours which had aroused "great public concern." Thus "nuisance" behaviours such as "shouting and swearing, hanging about and fooling around in groups, sometimes outside of other people"s homes..." were all defined as manifestations of antisocial behaviour (Audit Commission 1999: 13). However unacceptable such behaviours were, the report conceded that they were beyond the reach of the criminal justice system. The report also pointed to the significant problem posed by those young people "at risk" of engaging in crime. The report identified key groups of young offenders: "persistent offenders," young offenders "who have yet to develop an entrenched pattern of offending," "first time offenders," and, finally, "youth at risk," who "must be discouraged from getting involved in offending in the first place" (Audit Commission 1999: 13).

Risk identification was thus identified as an attempt to reduce offending among those already in the criminal justice system, and as a way of preventing others at risk of becoming criminals from entering this system.

Central to the interventionist project outlined in the report is a specific interpretation of the "causes of crime." For all practical purposes, this causal model reflected the conclusions drawn from the criminological research studies conducted by Professor David Farrington of the Cambridge Institute of Criminology (see Farrington 1994, 1996). Drawing directly on Farrington"s work, the report concluded that "high risk factors" include

> ...gender, with boys more likely to offend than girls; inadequate parenting, aggressive and hyperactive behaviour in early childhood; truancy and exclusion from school; peer group pressure to offend, unstable living conditions; lack of training and employment; and drug and alcohol abuse. (Audit Commission 1999: 58).

This long list of "causal factors" derives mainly from the multifactorial studies of crime conducted by Farrington in his longitudinal study of over four hundred "traditional" working-class boys. Beginning in 1961, the study traversed every conceivable aspect of the boys" social and personal lives: from family circumstances, income, family size, employment, and child rearing practices, to school performance, truancy, and interpersonal behaviour (Farrington 1994). As the Audit Commission (1999: 58) report put it:

> Those who experience many or all of these factors throughout their childhood and teenage years are at the highest risk of getting caught up in the cycle of antisocial behaviour, including offending which is then difficult to break. Those who start offending at an early age are more likely to become persistent offenders.

Although Farrington claimed that no single factor or even cluster of factors could necessarily guarantee the onset of offending, the various relational dynamics occurring in the context of "the family" were seen as central to explanations of crime creation:

> ...the presence of adverse family background (poor parental supervision, cruel, passive or neglecting attitude of the mother, parental conflict) doubled the presence of a later juvenile conviction...we can now show that family factors predict delinquency independently of other factors (Farrington 1994: 11).

Despite Farrington"s failure to clearly define the various terms used to describe aspects of family functioning, and the corresponding danger of imposing middle-class values and standards on working-class people, his conclusions are given a thorough and entirely uncritical airing by the Audit Commission (1999: 62), which claimed, for example, that

> [i]nadequate parenting is strongly associated with later offending. Neglect by parents, poor maternal and domestic care before the age of five years, insecure attachment, family conflict, and the absence of a good relationship with either parent have all been shown to increase the risk of behaviour problems and subsequent offending.

Likewise, the Audit Commission (1999: 62) had no trouble in concluding, with all the authority of those possessed of certainty, that

> Young people who say that their attachment to their family is weak, are most likely to report that they have committed offences, as are those who have experienced cruelty and abuse at the hands of parents. The nature of parental supervision is also important. Parents who rely heavily on harsh punishment, or who are erratic in their discipline, are twice as likely to have children who offend. Harsh punishment is also associated with more violent and frequent offending.

Significantly, this confidence and certainty is actually severely modified by the usual methodological scruples. Although the report "reveals" that family factors were most closely associated with longer-term offending, the task of "measuring" the impact of intra-family functioning on crime was decidedly difficult:

> Predicting the future behaviour of individuals is...closely linked to factors such as parental conflict and the quality of life in the early years, although these are...difficult to measure (Audit Commission 1999: 62).

The report further suggests that the risk of offending was higher in families with "poor disciplinary practices" and for those who lived in underprivileged neighbourhoods:

> Research has shown that children who are brought up in families with lax parental discipline and in a poor neighbourhood have a higher risk of becoming offenders (Audit Commission 1999: 62).

To support this claim, the report provided two shaded geographical maps detailing the statistical correlation between low-income areas and high crime in the West Midlands (Audit Commission 1999: 63). Yet, despite such confident identification of risk factors in "high-crime" areas, the report offered an important qualification:

> While it is useful to predict the local areas in which children are most likely to become delinquent—on the basis of family size, social status and parental separation—these factors are also able to identify three quarters of individual offenders, *but they may overpredict fivefold* (Audit Commission 1999: 62) (Our emphasis).

As we note below, such considerations take on particular importance when we begin to unravel the various philosophical-cum-methodological assumptions relied upon by risk-based researchers. The need for caution when confronted by confident empirical conclusions becomes even more pressing when we consider the huge sums of public money devoted to British youth crime prevention programs. Indeed, the overarching program of intervention suggested by the Audit Commission involves a wide range of government departments, voluntary organisations, and other "agencies." The Audit Commission report asserts that the causal factors identified by researchers such as David Farrington

> ...can be used to help target measures to prevent crime by identifying areas where young people are at high risk. Steps can be taken by a wide range of agencies to address problems before those at risk start to offend. Such agencies would involve parents "who can be helped to bring children up to respect the law and the rights of other people," schools, social services, health, leisure services and youth services,

Risk and Crime Control: The British Experience

housing, training agencies, and drug and alcohol services (Audit Commission 1999: 59).

Particular emphasis is given in the report to "improving parenting":

> Parents who are bringing up their children in difficult circumstances can be helped by professionals (or by volunteer, experienced parents) to improve their partnering skills and produce better behaved, more trustworthy children who need less expensive supervision and intervention later on....Parent education aims to help parents develop self-awareness and self-confidence and improves their capacity to support and nurture their children (Audit Commission 1999: 63).

To facilitate improved parenting skills, the report recommended a range of support initiatives, including family centres (staffed by multiagency workers), volunteer networks, and a host of other "nurturing" approaches. It was also recommended that social services, health services, education departments, and other organisations ought to pilot support and parent skill-training schemes in "deprived areas." Under the guidance of child and adolescent mental health workers, parents were urged to involve their "at-risk children" in a host of learning tasks such as helping them "solve problems" in "structured ways." Parents are further urged to improve disciplinary techniques and communication processes.

Evaluation of such initiatives should, according to the commission, be undertaken in order to establish whether parenting skills have improved and whether this has altered the behaviours of children and young people deemed to be at risk of offending. The commission reiterated this recommendation, suggesting that any program of intervention should be *targeted*, and, most importantly, that this should take place as early as possible in the life of the child. This need for early intervention is imperative, because some of the damage may have been done inside the womb:

> It may be possible to identify children early on that could benefit from targeted help and thereby avoid problems later on. Characteristics such as low birth weight and having problems shortly after birth, poor performance in IQ test at age three, and early childhood behaviour, which is aggressive, hyperactive, impulsive or disruptive, are key identifiers. Health visitors are likely to have a key role in identifying the

local areas and families which may be most at risk" (Audit Commission 1999: 64).

"Structured" and "targeted" forms of early intervention were seen as most usefully applied in the context of nursery education. Thus, children should be exposed to preschool educational environments that are characterised by structured modes of learning, conducive staff-pupil ratios, and, of course, more research to evaluate whether all this works in terms of bringing up more socially acceptable, conformist, and law-abiding children. Local authorities should be actively involved in "targeting schemes to provide intensive, structured pre-school education and home support for three or four year olds, in which parents are involved, to areas of high risk and deprivation, and they should be evaluated" (Audit Commission 1999: 65).

In addition to the promotion of services to tackle "school misbehaviour," truancy, and drug and alcohol problems, the report recommends greater cooperation among key institutions involved in the "socialisation" of young people. Moreover, the work of institutions, such as families, schools, religious institutions and community organisations should be aimed at ensuring that "children have the opportunity to become responsible and capable citizens" (Audit Commission 1999: 94).

In detailing a strategy to reduce risk among certain cohorts of children and young people, the authors of the report recommended a coordinated response by local authorities and central government departments. They placed less emphasis on criminal justice measures to deal with crime and more on the "targeting of preventive services to deprived areas, piloting and evaluation of preventive services and local coordination to prevent youth crime" (1999). While the authors of the report urge consultation with those living in "areas of highest risk," and the active inclusion of the "community" in any program of intervention, the overriding aim of the project "should be" to develop programs designed to "address risk factors known to be associated with offending" (Audit Commission 1999: 100).

Putting Theory into Practice

At least in the eyes of the Blair government and readers of the tabloid press, the Audit Commission and the Youth Justice Task

Force provided the right kind of foundation for a long-awaited overhaul of the juvenile justice system in Britain. Drawing on criminological research and "evidence-based" programs of intervention, the new system was to rely on a coordinated range of activities designed to diminish the level of risk among certain categories of young people—mostly from "deprived areas."

The resulting legislation was the *Crime and Disorder Act 1998*. This act provided for the creation of a Youth Justice Board designed to advise the Home Secretary on the progress of the youth justice system, and to monitor the general performance of the system as well as to advise the Home Secretary on national standards. These standards would help to shape the work of newly created multdisciplinary Youth Justice Teams and to ensure the evaluation of programs and the enhancement of "good practice."

Chaired by Lord Warner of Brockley, the work of the Youth Justice Board was underscored by a commitment to "early intervention in the lives of young people," the creation of effective and localised systems of youth justice, "strong intervention" by the board when local agencies are failing, and a general coordinated approach across government to "tackle offending as an urgent priority" (Youth Justice Board 2001: 1).

By overseeing the creation of a new regime of youth justice (based heavily on proposals set out in *Misspent Youth*), the board gave full expression to a reinvigorated commitment to a philosophy of rehabilitation. As Pitts (2001: 25) comments:

> Whereas the rehabilitative techniques of the 1960s had aimed to ameliorate emotional and social deprivation, this new approach to rehabilitation aimed to restructure the modes of thought, the values, the attitudes and the behaviours of young offenders, the control strategies of their parents and the classroom regimes presided over by their teachers. While presenting themselves as new forms of rehabilitation, these techniques were straightforwardly "correctional" in both intent and content.

The new system of justice set out in the *Crime and Disorder Act 1998* established a wide range of new penalties aimed at both young offenders and their parents. Parent Orders provided for programs designed to enhance parenting skills. (In 1999 over 1,100 Parent Orders were granted by the courts). Anti-Social Behaviour Orders, Child Safety Orders and provisions for local curfews were established as "preemptive" crime control measures. Final warnings and Reprimands constituted the basis of pre-court, "last-ditch" interventions, while a range of noncustodial penalties and semi-indeterminate Detention and Training Orders formed the core of the new schedule of court-administered penalties. Custodial and noncustodial provisions contained in the Act allowed for the blending of a range of sentencing rationalities such as retribution, deterrence, and rehabilitation–all aimed at the primary goal of preventing and/or reducing offending among "at-risk" youth.

The work of the Youth Justice Board was concerned most closely with noncustodial penalties and the development and implementation of programs aimed at those children, young people, and their families deemed "at risk." The work of the board was pitched primarily at primary and secondary levels of crime prevention through interventions designed to alleviate the predispositional conditions associated with offending. The design of the new system seems to have taken into account the Bonnemaison program in France, the Perry Pre-school project in North America, and the Pathways to Prevention program in Australia. This is especially so given the way the Youth Justice Board presided over a vast interlocking network of initiatives, activities, and interventions all "targeted" at young people and families in "high-crime," "deprived" areas.

The financial costs of such a program have proved to be considerable. For example, in 1999 the Youth Justice Board allocated 2.28 million pounds to forty new education and training programs, 23 million pounds to Youth Justice Teams in order to recruit new specialist drug workers, and 2 million pounds for twenty-four "behavioural programs."

In 1999, funding was also provided for seventy Youth Inclusion Programs in the most deprived areas in England and Wales. These programs were targeted at young people deemed to be "at risk" because of drug and alcohol abuse and provided for a range of specifically tailored education and skills-based programs. By summer 2000, there were over two hundred Youth Inclusion Programs in existence with over 20,000 young people involved in various programs. In a press release, the Youth Justice Board boasted that 102 Youth Inclusion Programs in the most deprived areas took up 591,818 hours of young people"s time with a further 35,000 hours of volunteer time devoted to these projects (Youth

Justice Board 2001: 1). The board further claimed that its programs had a significant impact in terms of crime reduction among young people: 36 percent reduction in house burglaries and an 18 percent reduction in the general level of youth crime.

Primary responsibility for the implementation of plans to address the problems experienced by at-risk children and young people was given to locally based Youth Justice Teams. Comprised of staff seconded from the police, probation service education, social services, the health service, and occasionally, the youth services and volunteer workers, these teams role, was to establish a comprehensive Youth Offender Plan. The brief for this plan was that it should establish and coordinate a range of services for at-risk children, young people, and their families. Framed in an epistemological context structured around the developmental theories of criminologists such as Farrington, as well as recommendations contained in official government reports, the planned charged the Youth Justice Teams with the responsibility of developing "early, targeted intervention to deal with anti-social behaviour and divert young people from crime" (Youth Justice Board 2001: 2).

A key element in this approach was the use of "cognitive skills training." Designed to alter the "criminogenic" values and attitudes of actual and/or potential offenders, early intervention programs were required to address both the biological and psychological factors that appeared to predispose some individuals to offending. These factors included everything from low birth weight and low IQ to "aggressivity" or "impulsivity," as well as the intra-familial conditions associated with "poor parenting." Cognitive skills training would be used specifically to address the values, attitudes, and worldviews of those deemed at risk. Individual counselling, group work, and an assortment of community-based programs were proposed to achieve this goal.

The nature and scope of activities overseen by the Youth Justice Board and implemented "on the ground" by Youth Justice Teams is awe-inspiring. Even more awesome is the amount of government funds invested in supporting the range of interventionist programs. Based on a philosophical platform of the programs that seeks to get "tough on crime," the challenges facing the new architects and practitioners of youth crime control are daunting. They are especially daunting given the assumptions upon which this whole program rests.

The trajectory set for this interventionist project derives from a set of narrow and highly dubious assumptions about the origins of criminal and "antisocial" behaviour. The mélange of factors used to explain crime derives from traditions of criminological inquiry that have long been characterised by the belief that criminal activity could be explained directly by reference to a range of *measurable* individual, familial, and social factors. In developing a critique of this perspective, we draw attention to the essential and essentialising elements of youth crime prevention discourses that underpin interventionist programs in a number of English-speaking Western countries (Hogg and Brown 1998).

The Role of Science—Once More

The theoretical foundations of New Labour"s approach to juvenile justice are deeply problematic. These foundations are alive and well in the work of developmental criminologists such as David Farrington, who maintain that the essential factors linking some young people to crime can be "scientifically" mapped via processes of classification, measurement, and interpretation. Crime and its supposed "causes" are thus objectified phenomena amenable to the systematic application of "scientific method." The analyses of regression, correlation, and deviation are the methodological props upon which this elaborate investigative process is built.

Inevitably, this kind of research identifies an array of "explanatory" or dispositional factors, some of which may or may not be associated with offending. Farrington himself, as well as others such as his mentor Donald West (1982), readily admit that they cannot accurately predict which factors in whichever permutation can "trigger" offending. As Utting (1994: 18) argues:

> It is important to recognize that...attempts to target and stigmatize young children as potential offenders using statistical predictors are likely to misidentify a proportion of children who will not turn to crime, while missing many others who are equally at risk.

In effect, this means that even in their own terms, using all the sophisticated methodological techniques available to them, these researchers can never claim predictive certainty. While "margins of error" are certainly part of the explanatory armory of positivistic researchers, the fact remains that the intervention strategies mounted to confront crime among young people are, at best, based on inaccurate forecasts of who should or should not be "targeted." Further, as Pitts (2001: 12) observes:

> ...if we are unable to accord some degree of causal primacy to "parenting", "truancy", "drug abuse", "homelessness" and the like, to theories of the ways in which these correlates interact, we are little nearer understanding the causes of youth crime and our choice of methods of intervention [is] haphazard. In the event, a process of political and scientific attrition has resolved this, by no means insignificant, problem.

By laying claim to a "scientific status"—where the idea of "science" clearly draws on the legitimacy and the accomplishments of the natural sciences—multifactorial research effectively serves to legitimate, at least from a governmental perspective, a plethora of interventions whose explanatory powers are actually highly dubious. The kinds of scientific method involved here, with its celebration of impartiality and objectification, provide a convenient way of screening out alternative explanations of crime and its causes. For instance, critical theories that raise awkward questions about the categories employed in risk-based approaches, and the skewed focus on particular sorts of risk, find little or no expression in official British reports on youth crime. Instead, reports such as *Misspent Youth* devote their pages to countless and repetitious statements that dwell on a selective range of "factors" that appear to correlate with crime.

Reductionism

Perhaps more concerning from a theoretical point of view is the failure of developmental researchers to incorporate any kind of theoretical reflexivity into their explanatory frameworks. Central to their analytic endeavors are a range of categories that purport to either "describe" or "explain" the nature and causes of juvenile offending. For example, as we have already explained in regard to the Australian case study, the category of "crime" is used uncritically to refer to rates of offending calculated by official governmental agencies. No effort is made to question these sources or indeed the fact that they are based on a variety of practices such as highly differential policing practices which precisely target the activities of young immigrant or working-class people. Corporate crime, white-collar crime, and the crimes of the rich and powerful are effectively screened out of this analytical exercise.

Instead, crime is equated with the actions of the inner-urban poor and disadvantaged. *Misspent Youth* reinforces this impression through its focus on "high crime areas" and "deprived areas." Such views dovetail neatly with wider discourses that correlate the "crime problem" with particular sections of society, most notably the "underclass" or, in the current British governmental vernacular, "socially excluded" populations.

In effect, crime is reduced to an "individualistic" account of human behaviours for which "the individual" that is, the poor, working-class male and immigrant, must be held "responsible." Such time-honoured accounts underpin a range of intervention strategies designed to alter the attitudes and behaviours of "at-risk" individuals. "Cognitive skills training" and other tailored interventions are used as dissuasive instruments in the battle against antisocial and criminogenic tendency. In this way it is assumed that if those "at risk" can think "straight," they will go "straight" (Pitts 2001: 30).

This simplistic, and yet immensely popular, approach rests on dubious and antiquated ideas about the origins of crime and the prospects for its prevention/reduction. As Pitts (2001: 30) argues:

> In so reasoning, the purveyors of cognitive skills training, like the eighteenth century Classicists, conflate rational/logical thinking with moral/law-abiding thinking; in so doing commit a categorical error since they fail to distinguish between the cognitive machinery which enables logical thought, and the ethical choices made possible by a capacity for logical thought. The assumption that people engage in crime because they lack capacity for logical thought is, at least, tendentious since, in reality, people often resort to crime, violence or deception because, in the circumstances in which they find themselves, it "works" for them.

The failure to consider either the social relations or the choices and practices which "at-risk youth" engage in characterises a lot of the British risk-based explanations of juvenile offending. Additionally, the heavy emphasis given to family and individual factors is achieved at the expense of an effort to theorise the complex connections between issues of inequality, poverty, and policing. At best, such factors are lightly sketched onto the background. The origins of crime are not seen to be completely unrelated to government polices and regulatory practices, but rather are said to lie firmly with the "deficits" that beset particular "types" of young people and their families.

Conclusion

Interventionist "solutions" to a narrowly conceived "crime problem" are necessarily hinged, according to a developmental perspective, on a broad range of programs aimed at addressing the deficits of certain population groups.

Misspent Youth, for example, proposes a bold and expensive interdepartmental and multidisciplinary program of intervention which, through the management of the Youth Justice Board and, at "ground zero," through the operations of Youth Justice Teams, has resulted in significant points of contact between practitioners and those at risk. Targeted interventions, however, are directed specifically at individual deficiencies exhibited by parents and young people. For the former, this may mean "parenting skills" programs and, for the latter, "cognitive skills training."

Administered by a new cadre of Youth Justice Workers, as well as by a small army of education, health, and welfare specialists, these programs are reminiscent of earlier interventions in which selected families from the "lower orders" taught how to be good parents and responsible citizens through the Settlement House programs (Benjamin, Bessant, and Watts 1997). This similarly ensures they come to appreciate middle-class values and conform to appropriate codes of behaviour (Hunt 1999). "Appropriate" child-rearing practices, application of normative practices of care and supervision, and the promotion of more "effective" forms of "communication" between parents and their children are central to this project. Family-oriented interventions derive, of course, from the epistemological foundations upon which the work of the Youth Justice Board and Youth Justice Teams are based.

Thus, although the Youth Justice Board established a battery of programs to assist young people and their families in avoiding the prospect of crime, little or no attention has been drawn to how the "big questions" (e.g., poverty) typically associated with such behaviour might be addressed. Poverty, deprivation, and disadvantage are mentioned only as key correlates of crime. Yet, there is no mention of specific proposals relating to how, precisely, such "problems" might be alleviated. Instead, the emphasis in *Misspent Youth* rests on behaviour modification and attitudinal change. Indeed, as Pitts (forthcoming: 13—14) rightly points out, there is a significant body of empirical work which demonstrates that serious juvenile offending may be correlated far more closely with "neighborhood" factors rather than parenting issues per se. Given the claims of many risk-based researchers about causal links between poverty and crime, and given government commitments to reduce the number of youth at risk, it does seem very odd that issues of poverty, disadvantage, poor housing, education, inadequate leisure and recreation facilities, and lack of support services are largely ignored (Wikstrom and Loeder 1997; Pitts and Hope 1988; Young 1999; Jones 2001).

Chapter Six: Governance of Social Problems and Problem Populations

A city is composed of different kinds of men: similar people cannot bring a city into existence.
(Aristotle, The Politics)

The 1980s and 1990s can be characterised by a popular and academic preoccupation with the threat that "delinquent" and "criminally inclined" young people were said to pose to social order (Davis 1992). There is a long history of "moral panics" about "hooligans" (Pearson 1983) and larrikins in the nineteenth century, and, since the 1950s about "youth cultures" such as "bodgies and widgies," "punks," "goths," etc. The search for solutions to various "youth-related" problems has been most marked in relation to crime and public disorder.

Moral panics over juvenile crime have invariably been accompanied by an often frenzied search for solutions (Simpson 1997). The moral panics, however, have undergone a transformation over the past few decades from discourses about "maladjusted youth" informed by a sociology of deviance to the new scientific-legal representation of them as being "at risk" (Rose 1990, 1996). Contemporary risk rhetoric now hinges more on the factors that predispose some young people rather than others to a life of crime. In adopting a multifactoral assessment of levels, types, and inventories of risk, the researcher hopes to establish a predictive, a loose causal map or grid to calibrate the likelihood of offending in any given circumstance. It is then the responsibility of policy makers and practitioners, those at the interventionist "coal face," to develop specific programs to address and overcome the risk factors.

Whatever else it achieves, risk-based research informs practices that promote a more intensive focus on the behaviours of targeted groups of juvenile offenders and their families. Aboriginal offenders and those from the "badlands" of "the urban poor" come in for the closest scrutiny (Carrington 1993). One of the outcomes of risk-based interventions is that, despite acknowledging the effects of "social" or "environmental" factors, they are invariably directed toward the objective of correcting the individual via incursions into their everyday lives.

In stressing the intellectual framework of the science of risk and the ways certain styles of reasoning are set loose, we should not forget then that there are numerous practical consequences. The emergence of risk discourses over the past two decades has produced a heightened concern about criminal, antisocial, and delinquent young people. One consequence is new management tasks prescribed by the "science of risk" fore-shadowing extensive and frequent interventions across the lifecycle.

Government of the Young Person

Whose conduct have the various processes of government set out to govern? A central problem of government has always been represented in terms of "class," though the government of problems emerging from age cohorts and gender has never been far behind, giving rise to concerns about social problems such as poverty, unemployment, and working-class crime.

In the nineteenth century it was the "dangerous classes" who were identified as responsible for crime. Today, the "underclass" can be just as readily invoked as the source of all our contemporary social problems (White 1994a, 1994b; Vinson 1999). As Pearson (1983) points out, the fears of the "respectable middle classes" have long been translated into both empirical scientific enquiry into what the "lower orders" are doing as well as persistent correctionalist and welfarist projects designed to limit the damage they can do to "society." The empirico-positivist gaze has remained steady in this regard as have the subtle undertones of eugenicist thought running through the history of such discursive practices and research projects.

The restructuring of Australia"s labour market and the near-complete collapse of the full-time youth labour market (Wooden 1998: 35) in particular, have provided a context for a burgeoning academic interest in "the youth problem" as well as a context in which public anxieties about young people have flourished.[1] The undoubted problem of youth unemployment has been a major contributing factor in recurrent "moral panics" about the specter of a youth "underclass" of unemployed, homeless and marginalised young people (White 1994a; Rutter, Giller, and Hagill 1998).

This is another way of saying that public concern about "at-risk" young people owes much to the publicity given to research or to discussion and speculation by the media, politicians, and social commentators. Public concern over issues such as juvenile crime has been sufficient to generate a powerful mix of anxiety and public outrage. To a large extent, the media has been operating as an agent of moral indignation in serving to shape and define the social problem of youth at risk. The vocabulary used in media and popular reports on what are known by researchers as "youth at risk" reflects arguments about a decline in moral standards and the demise of civilised society (Eckersley 1992, 1993). These discussions have typically selected out youth unemployment, youth homelessness, youth suicide, juvenile delinquency/crime, and drug addiction as core problems.

Such concerns are not new. Much of the new risk talk begins with a discussion about the deteriorating socioeconomic environment. It is argued that young people now encounter "new morbidities" that present major obstacles to becoming adult. Batten and Russell"s (1995: 1) position is typical:

> The term "at risk"...is used to describe or identify young people who, beset by particular difficulties and disadvantages, are thought likely to fail to achieve the development in their adolescent years that would provide a sound basis for a satisfying and fulfilling adult life.

These new concerns have fitted seamlessly into much older discourses about the necessary and "normal" steps all young people must take if they are to achieve a "normal," "mature" adult status (Griffin 1993). The development of life course theory and research over the twentieth century has been used to reassure us that there are "normal" developmental steps, cognitive skills, and social accomplishments (all set against age rankings) which, it is argued, can be accurately measured to determine how well individuals are travelling down their path toward an inevitable rendezvous with responsible adulthood.

Schools and New Modes of Governance

Education institutions have developed into key sites for identifying and monitoring "youth at risk of unemployment" and for providing points of entry for intervention into their lives.

Schools also offer an ideal site because most young people are required by law to pass through the system.

Education institutions have become critical for the management of youth "at risk" of unemployment. This is evident, not only by the implementation of education policies since the 1970s directed toward encouraging young people to remain in education institutions, but also more recently by the introduction of the Department of Social Securities" Common Youth Allowance (Edwards, Howard, and Miller 2001). These new arrangements make receipt of income support conditional on the young person"s return to school or to some form of training.

The durability of this confidence in approach that worked for an industrial society, in conjunction with increasing credentialism and political imperatives to "soak up" the unemployed, means education institutions such as schools, TAFE colleges, and universities have become liferafts on a sea of hopeful imaginings about their ability to reconstruct a secure society like the one we "remember."

The increased responsibilities for education institutions include having to

- compensate for the "failure" of "the family" as well as for the collapse of the full-time labour markets
- address new "problems" allegedly created by the "breakdown" of "the family" and young people"s inability to obtain full-time employment

The category of "youth at risk" has seen this extension of governance through the education system. Dryfoos"s vision of what she calls a "one-stop" service that extends throughout the education system of a variety of human services directed to other aspects of one"s life is illustrative of a progressive or benevolent method for extending the governance of young people, and through them, of their families. Turning schools into "one-stop centres" provides direct access to students on a daily basis so that their educational, physical, psychological, and social needs are addressed in a "rational, holistic fashion." Facilitating this through the schools is intended to "relieve the burden" on "society" by changing high-risk behaviours (Dryfoos 1996:1).

Bypassing Nostalgia

In effect, one response to the consequences of the breakdown of the traditional industrial order has been to retreat into the past by fortifying many of the institutions that were central to that order. The strategy of keeping most young people in some form of education/training for as long as possible as a solution for "youth at risk" is a classic example of a response informed by older modes of thinking and acting to solve problems occurring within what Beck (1992) has called a "risk society."

While much of the rhetoric about the contemporary role of education talks about embracing change, what we are seeing involves resistance to change. As Lowenthal explains, harking back to the past often happens in hard times; indeed, disillusionment with the present "can induce a dangerous addiction with the visible past" (1995). Similarly, Franklin (1998: 2) points out that this response builds on idealised notions of community and encourages efforts to bring back "the family," reconstruct neighbourhoods, and reassert a commonsense morality to create the solidarity we once "knew." We see this in the requirement that education institutions become frontline responses to unemployment (Bessant 1995).

Schools have been called on to develop strategies that would stop students "at risk" from leaving school "early." As Sweet (1998: 12) notes:

> This priority has seen substantial effort and expenditure put into successive initiatives such as the Australian Trainee Scheme, Career Start Traineeships, the Australian Vocational Certificate, the Modern Australian Apprenticeship and Trainee System and New Apprenticeships....Successive governments have been increasing access to such employment-based structured training opportunities as a key strategy in increasing young people"s access to vocational education and training and in combating the difficulties that they face in the labour market.

Encouraging young people toward vocational education has been a government priority. As Sweet notes:

> Increasing young people"s participation in vocational education and training has been one of the central priorities of government during the 1990s. Between 1989—90 and 1995—96 government expenditure on

TAFE increased by 21 percent in real terms, from $1.9 billion to $2.6 billion (Sweet 1998: 11).

Yet, schools are institutions of the old industrial order, and despite the recent restructuring, they remain very much the product of that old order, and, says Beck, this "is doomed to fail" (Beck 1998: 9—22). The politics of these orthodox responses mean we will stay bound to industrial notions of "progress." The belief that the risks we face—such as unemployment—can be tamed by reclaiming industrial institutions and nineteenth century models of hazard assessment may prove sadly inadequate.

If we are to respond effectively to change, and specifically to the problems resulting from the shift toward a postindustrial, post-full employment society, we need to ask whether we are addressing the actual causes of problems such as unemployment. Framing the problem in terms of "youth at risk" effectively renegs on the opportunity to address the actual causes of unemployment.

Although critics of national employment policy since the 1980s have called for more jobs, the number of new jobs required to meet the needs of young people—and others—wanting jobs remains insufficient. The political resistance on the part of business and other elite groups to investment in the public sector has been one major constraint. The private sector, unlikely in the foreseeable future to alter its preference for "downsizing" so as to preserve its profit line, has been another.

What we are seeing with the category of "youth at risk of unemployment" is an attempt by proponents to force a relatively new development (a restructured labour market) into an old paradigm which takes industrial culture as a "given." So we observe attempts to discover the causes and/or indicators of "youth at risk" (of unemployment) without considering the possibility that a new set of theoretical, philosophical, ethical, and practical paradigms is required.

According to Beck, industrial society and full employment have been dependent on the unequal positions of men and women, but the dynamics of individualisation which accompanied this means that people have been progressively removed from the traditional "constraints of gender." Under conditions of modernity, for example, women have been released from their ascribed roles (i.e., as mother/wife) in search of "a life of their own." This "liberation," however, has *not* occurred with young people, indeed, we observe the opposite—"increased governance." Modernisation not only dissolves the notion of full-time waged labour, it also directly challenges many of the "givens" of industrial culture (Beck 1992).

Instead of insisting on returning most/all young people to institutions (such as schools) as a "solution" to youth unemployment, perhaps it is more productive to ask questions such as the following:

- In a context of material abundance, and a decline in the demand for human labour, can we separate income from waged labour?
- How can we provide the fundamental experiences once inherent in the young person"s initial work experiences?
- Besides full-time waged work, what opportunities can we develop to help facilitate a young person"s identity formation?
- Surely we must ask: Given the changes that have taken place, on what basis are young people going to receive an income? And, how are young people going to participate in those fundamental experiences previously provided by waged work?

We now see the new labour systems emerging that remove the traditional risks of a scarcity of work. This is not a bad thing if it is handled thoughtfully. Beck argues that these labour systems redistribute and transform unemployment into a developmental productive force. According to Beck, "the risks accompanying the forms of under-employment compete with the partial freedom and sovereignty gained in being able to arrange their own lives" (Beck 1992: 148).

At the same time that underemployment challenges the individual, it also presents new questions about the models of social order and social integration we have traditionally relied on—and which are deeply inscribed into the social sciences.

From Intervention to Crime Prevention

There is one other distinctive implication of the new science of risk discourse. Like the older "sociology of deviance," the primary business of the sociology of risk involves what Foucault referred to as "dividing practices" that distinguish in this instance between those who are at risk of certain "problems" and those who are not. While most "risk" research gives the impression of distinguishing between those "at risk" and "the rest," the "youth-at-risk" category differs from older categories of the delinquent, in terms of its capacity to potentially incorporate the entire population of young people.

It is also fair to note that its actual effect to date has been a continuation of criminology"s traditional preoccupation with "the coloured," "the poor," or "working-class people," that is, all those who in Hagan and McCarthy"s (1997) hateful phrase, make up the "surplus population." As such, risk-based research is part of a disciplinary practice that involves marking out those viewed as posing an actual or potential threat to social order and applying regulatory strategies to them.

The authors of the *Pathways to Prevention* report, for example, insist that it is worth concentrating on "investment in child-friendly" institutions and communities, and the *manipulation of multiple risk and predictive factors* at crucial transition points, such as at around birth, the preschool years, the transition from primary to high school, and the transition from high school to higher education or the workforce (National Crime Prevention 1999: 10). The main aim is to intervene and intervene early at each major stage in a young person"s life. The *Pathways to Prevention* report states that

> ...developmental prevention involves intervention early in the developmental pathways that lead to crime and substance abuse.

Thus, it is suggested that "intervention can occur most effectively" at each "transition point" in a young person"s formative years (National Crime Prevention 1999: 10). Intervention, according to the report, needs to be tailored to the particular circumstances facing each child at various transition points so as to offset the consequences of "cumulative risk" (National Crime Prevention 1999: 11). Early intervention, in the *strategic* rather than strictly chronological sense, is thus crucial to the preventive process. The primary rationale, however, is to intervene "early" (a preemptive strike as it were) in the developmental process, presumably well before any signs of criminal or delinquent behaviour arise.

The quandary here is that if it is not possible to identify the *precise* likelihood of those who may or, equally, may not engage in offending, then how should a "targeted" program of intervention be mounted? A blanket approach to intervention, implicit in much of the report, would intervene in the lives of all those deemed at risk, irrespective of whether those young people have or have not actually offended. Faced with such a problem, the architects of crime prevention may suggest scales, grids, maps, or inventories that differentiate between types of risk. But which factors take precedence in any analytical explanation? Or are they to be regarded as equally important? Is it possible to target those most at risk? How does risk apply to those from middle-class or affluent backgrounds who may, in various ways, be more protected from the reach of the state?

These are both technical and theoretical questions that intrude into any risk management approach to crime prevention. Ethical and moral questions also arise in relation to the promotion of greater state intervention, often for no other reason than that it is deemed "necessary" by the state. What, say, do "at-risk" populations get in the quest to prevent crime? Why should the state gaze so intensely on some of our most vulnerable and powerless populations? Why is the scrutiny so partial and based on a narrowly conceived "crime problem"? Why has the *Pathways to Prevention* report so studiously avoided addressing these questions?

The likely outcome of the developmental strategies proposed by the *Pathways* report is the creation of a vast army of accredited professional personnel dedicated to the task of helping to reduce crime through countless programs, domiciliary visits, and other forms of intervention. Implicitly, interventionism is celebrated for its own sake as something necessary and good for those deemed "at risk." State intervention for purposes of restoring social order or ensuring normative acquiescence is something working-class families have been historically familiar with (Rose 1998). Yet, while such interventionism is proposed as a "good practice," its documented history shows a litany of intrusive, coercive, and regulatory recollections on the part of those subject to the attentions of state-sponsored officials. Crime prevention becomes simply the latest in a long line of disciplinary strategies evoked to legitimate increased official intervention into the lives of some of society"s most vulnerable members.

Simply put, the arguments presented in such projects are not persuasive. The economic/social outcomes likely to emerge from the proposed projects are minimal; indeed, we have concerns that the policies and practices likely to result can have a damaging impact on the lives of the young people, their families, and the local communities deemed to be at risk. It would be encouraging to see an acknowledgment of arguments that the interventions that risk-based projects such as the Sibling Study and *Pathways to Prevention* report are designed to produce will not necessarily improve individual or social life (see Rose 1994; Danziger 1990).

Through these risk-based assessments, researchers promise early-warning systems that identify the defiled and/or injured young people who have become public liabilities and hence of limited capital value. Once identified, they are promptly directed into processes of containment where they are treated, classified, frequently incarcerated, and in due time regulated into responsible adult life. There appears to be no awareness in the documentation of what may be politically, socially, and ethically problematic about the project.

More efficient case management is one of the intended outcomes of this risk-based research. Indeed, case management is one of the most convenient and effective intervention strategies available to workers (especially in the current managerialist climate). The usefulness of case management lies in its capacity to individualise intervention through the application of "customised" programs and practices. As we indicate below, the articulation of risk to practice is completed through a process grounded in concerns about correction or normalisation.

Here we see disciplinary power in action, centred around and reliant upon the notion of docile bodies. The Sibling Study is aimed toward disciplining the body in ways that provide a submissive, productive, and well-adjusted young person. Those young people judged to be "at risk" thereby become objects of scientific study and expert management, as they are implicated in networks of power relations that discipline unruly forces seen to ruin chances of their normalisation.

Conclusion

These risk-based studies are blind to the role of policing in constructing the "crime problem" and to the wider contexts of social and economic decline that bear down on young people and their families. The privatisation of responsibility for the welfare and education of young people is simply overlooked in this risk-based research. There is no consideration of the fact that since the early 1980s millions of dollars have been taken from the public and community sectors for the care, protection, and education of young people—a withdrawal justified in terms of a "necessity" to deal with fiscal debt. This is honoured in conjunction with the new doctrines of limited collective responsibility (O"Neill 1994). Ignored is the general shift in thinking about public spending that dictates provision for basics. Institutions such as schools, health care and social security are cut and substituted with more prisons and police. The way in which our submission to market-generated values, outlooks, and imperatives has restricted options to protect, care for, and educate children and young people is omitted from the analysis.

For example, if we are going to talk about risk, could it be argued that the liberal notion of the individual as the basic social/market unit is what locates many young people in various states of precarious vulnerability and thereby places them in greatest risk? If we agree for a moment to accept risk-based researchers" dubious arguments about social inheritance; if we accept arguments about the intergenerational transmission of underclass lifestyles, etc., then why don"t these argument apply to the idea that poor public health and an impoverished education and welfare system also form a critical part of the legacy inherited by succeeding generations?

The omission of these factors in the analysis of "youth at risk" is a staggering indictment of what seems to be a preoccupation with the need to identify more traditional individual-centred causes of juvenile crime.

Indeed, such questions intrude upon the fixed gaze of empirical science, which is earnestly devoted to the process of identification and classification. Sadly also, the predictive quality of empirical studies is often very disappointing (Utting 1994)—a point confirmed by the qualified doubts of some of the most well-known of blunderbuss investigators (Farrington 1994).

Also of concern are the likely outcomes of such representations of "youth at risk" on relations between older people (i.e., law enforcement officers, teachers, parents, etc.) and young people. Because the way we see things effects our responses, especially in terms of problem solving, these approaches to understanding young people cause considerable damage to our capacities to relate with, and make sense of, young people.

These dividing practices reinforce older notions of adjustment and what we can expect in terms of the transition to the development of adult capabilities. They reinforce the "normal process" of socially necessary and psychologically inevitable adolescent maturation into a successful adult role. They define gradations of "maladaptive" or risky behaviours through the deployment of "psychosocial models" to "diagnose" the early "symptoms" of "dysfunctional youth," now called "youth at risk."

This apparent "necessity" to portray "youth at risk" as foreign or different from "us" enhances their transgressive status, which inhibits the capacity of many adult experts to relate effectively with those young people. If the objective of such risk-based research is to intervene with effective outcomes, then it is imperative to resist the tendency to portray young people as though they were some rare subdivision of humanity whose behaviours enable us to understand and respond to them in terms of where they fit in the matrix of types.

Note

[1] See Hogg and Brown 1998; Wyn and White 1997; Eckersley 1988; Eckersley 1992; Eckersley 1993; but cf. Sercombe 1997; Bessant and Hil 1997.

Conclusion

The social sciences have long maintained an interest in identifying and "knowing" the characteristics of certain "types" of young people. The primary business of disciplines such as sociology, psychology, criminology, etc. around "youth at risk" has been to catalogue, correlate, and classify the factors that distinguish actual or suspected "youth at risk" from the rest of the youth population (Rose 1990; Tait 1993; Bessant 1991, 1993, 1998; Kelly 1998). In methodological terms, the search for these distinguishing features is predicated on certain naturalist or objectivist assumptions essential to conventional social science.

In a period characterised by rapid and intense transformation, all this talk about "youth at risk of unemployment" serves to make us aware of the fact that widespread alarm on the part of adults about "idle youth" represents struggles over moral regulation of a section of the population that has long been seen as needing tight and proper management. Current discourses about "youth at risk of unemployment" (and associated problems) represent an effort to develop new ways of regulating "youth" at a particular historic juncture when rapid changes are taking place. These changes raise popular anxiety levels and are based on what is already known about "youth" as inherently or naturally deviant in a context characterised by the demise of traditionally commonly shared values that once guided conduct in conjunction with the dissolution of older forms of integration (i.e., family, community /clan) (Beck 1992).

The search for predicability, coherence, and objectivity in an uncertain world is a goal many social scientists continue to work hard to achieve. The job of verifying "the obvious" and confirming certain "apparent" "causal" connections depends on well-entrenched ontological, epistemological processes and assumptions about proper research methodology which have long been central to the empirical social sciences and closely connected to state-sponsored projects of governance.

Indeed, much of the contemporary research on "youth at risk" (of everything including unemployment) sanctions the further extension of the surveillance role of social science as it simultaneously annexes further the governmental project that has traditionally defined the character of our schooling system.

The critique developed here has been concerned with the processes of *categorisation* used to identify "troublesome youth." We have argued that the categories used in risk-based discourses are a powerful component of governmental processes that make it possible to identify sections of the youth population as the legitimate targets of state intervention. In the projects under scrutiny, we examine the way in which particular categorising processes are applied selectively to discrete sections of the youth population seen as responsible for the "crime problem." It is argued that the bodies of knowledge emanating from risk-based thinking rely on methodologies which support the idea that the "causes of crime" are located in the pathological makeup of the individual, his/her family, and/or immediate neighbourhood or "community."

We have argued that the central place given to risk-based thinking in juvenile justice is indicative of a more general trend toward increased governance of young people in advanced liberal democratic states. Indeed, the notion of risk has become the discursive conduit through which a range of disciplinary practices have been applied to particular "problem populations." Such has been the ascendancy of risk discourse over the past few years that it has become perhaps *the* major operational concept in most systems of Australian juvenile justice. It has found its way into most areas of policy and practice and is currently widely regarded as essential to any "targeted" and credible response to juvenile crime.

We have argued that the prescriptions for crime control being presented to Australian governments by the academics involved in the Pathways to Prevention project rely on a number of unquestioned and narrow assumptions about "crime" and "criminality" and how we know "crime." These assumptions about "crime" and "criminality" have for a long time sustained a "modernist criminology" in which conservative and progressive criminologists alike have been able to operate. We suggest that if the concept of "risk" has now come to dominate the problem-fixing agendas of many academics and government organisations, then this is not a concept to celebrate or a concept with which we can afford to be complacent.

Bibliography

Abbott, P. and Wallace, C., 1989, *The Family and the New Right*, Pluto Press: London.
Abbott-Chapman, J., Patterson, C., 1990, "Evaluation of the Students at Risk Program," in *Tasmanian Schools, Report 1*, Youth Education Studies Centre, Hobart.
ABS, 1998, *Australian Economic Indicators*, 1350.0 September, nos. 27 and 86.
Ainley, J., Batten, L., and Miller, H., 1984, *Patterns of Retention in Australian Government Schools*, ACER, Research Monograph no. 27, Hawthorn.
Allat, C., and Yeandle, S., 1992, *Youth Unemployment and the Family: Voices of Disordered Times*, Routledge: London.
Allen, J., 1998, *Response and Ability: Curriculum Package for Secondary Education on the Issue of Youth Suicide, Field Trial Manual 1 and 2*, Youth Suicide Prevention, National University Curriculum Project.
Anderson, D., 1979, "A Social—psychological Theory of School Drop Outs: An Exploratory Study," in G. Rowley (ed.), *Proceedings of the 1979 Annual Conference of AARE*, Melbourne, AARE: 282–94.
Anderson, N., 1923, *The Hobo: The Sociology of Homeless Men*, University of Chicago Press: Chicago.
Andreski, S., 1973, *Social Science as Sorcery*, Andre Deutsch: London.
Appleby, M., 1992, *Suicide Awareness Training Manual*, Rose Education Training Consultancy: Narellan.
Arblaster, A., 1984, *The Rise and Fall of Western Liberalism*, Oxford University Press: Oxford.
Aristotle, 1967, *The Politics* (trans. E.V. Rieu), Penguin: Harmondsworth.
Audit Commission 1999 *Misspent Youth: Young People and Crime*, The Audit Commission: London.
Australian Bureau of Statistics, 1998 *Economic Indicators* 1350.0 September.
Australian Curriculum Studies Association, 1992, *Measuring Up: Assessment, Evaluation and Educational Disadvantage*, ACT, Australian Curriculum Studies Association.
—————. 1996, *From Alienation to Engagement*, vols. 1, 2, and 3, ACSA Canberra.
Australian Education Council Review Committee (Finn Report), 1991, *Young People"s Participation in Post—compulsory Schooling: Report of the Australian Education Council Review Committee*, Australian Government Publishing Service: Canberra.
Batten, M., and Russell, J., 1995, *Students at Risk: A Review of Australian Literature 1980–1994*, ACER: Melbourne.
Batten, M., and Withers, G., 1995, *Programs for At-Risk Youth: A Review of the American, Canadian and British Literature Since 1984*, ACER: Camberwell.
Batten, M., Withers, G., Thomas, C., and McCurry, D., 1991, *Senior Students Now: The Challenges of Retention*, ACER: Hawthorn.
Bauman, Z., 1991, *Intimations of Postmodernity*, Routledge: London.
—————.1998, *Work, Consumption and the New Poor*, Open University Press: Buckingham.

Bibliography

Beautrais, A., Coggan, C., Fergusson, D., and Rivers, I., 1997, *The Prevention, Recognition and Management of Young People at Risk of Suicide: Development Guidelines for Schools*, New Zealand Ministry of Education and National Advisory Committee on Health and Disability.

Beck, U., 1992. *Risk Society: Towards a New Modernity*, Sage: London.

———.1997, *The Reinvention of Politics*, Polity Press: Cambridge.

———.1998, "Politics of Risk Society," in J. Franklin (ed.), *The Politics of Risk Society*, Polity Press: Cambridge.

———.1999, *World Risk Society*, Polity Press: Cambridge.

Beck, U., Giddens, A., and Lash., S., 1994, *Reflexive Modernisation*, Polity Press: Cambridge.

Bell, S., 1997, *Ungoverning the Economy*, Oxford University Press: Melbourne.

Benjamin, J., Bessant, J., Watts, R., 1997, *Making Groups Work*, Allen & Unwin: Sydney.

Bernstein, P., 1996, *Against the Gods: The Remarkable Story of Risk*, Wiley: New York.

Bessant, J., 1988, "Meeting the Demands of the Corporate Sector," in *Journal of Australian Studies*, no. 22, May 1988: 19–32.

———.1991, "Described, Measured and Labelled": Eugenics, Youth Policy and Moral Panic in Victoria in the 1950s," in B. Wilson and R. White (eds.), *For Their Own Good: Young People and State Intervention in Australia*, LaTrobe University Press, February 1991: 8–28.

———.1993, *Constituting Categories of Youth: Towards the Twenty-first Century*, Occasional Paper no. 3, National Centre for Socio-Legal Studies, LaTrobe University, October: 65.

———. 1995, The Discovery of an Australian "Juvenile Underclass," *Australian New Zealand Journal of Sociology*, vol. 31, no. 3: 32–48.

———. 1995, *Youth Unemployment and Crime: Policy, Work and the "Risk Society,"* Youth Research Centre, University of Melbourne: Melbourne.

———. 1998, "Meeting the Demands of the Corporate Sector," *Journal of Australian Studies*, no. 22, May: 19–32.

———. 2000, "Revising the Deficit Model: Youth at Risk in an Uncertain Labour Market," in J. Lee, B. Probert, and R. Watts (eds.), *Work in the New Economy: Policy, Programs, Populations*, Centre for Social Research: Melbourne: 236–55.

———. 2001, "From Sociology of Deviance to Sociology of Risk: Youth Homelessness and the Problem of Empiricism," *Journal of Criminal Justice: An International Journal*, vol. 29, no. 1, 31–44.

Bessant, J., and Hil, R., (eds.) 1997, *Youth Crime and the Media: Media Representations of and Reactions to Young People in Relation to Law and Order*, Australian Clearinghouse for Youth Studies.

Bessant, J., and Watts, R., 1996, "Young People with Hope: Responding to Cultural Pessimism," Australian Catholic University.

———. 1999, *Sociology Australia*, Allen & Unwin: Sydney.

Bledstein, B., 1976, *The Culture of Professionalism*, W.W. Norton: New York.

Blocker, L., and Copeland, E. P., 1994, "Determinants of Resilience in High Stressed Youth," *High School Journal*, vol. 77, No. 4: 286–93.

Blum, R., 1987, "Contemporary Threats to Adolescent Health in the United States," Journal of the American Medical Association, vol. 257, no. 24: 33–45.

Bibliography

Bourdieu, P. et al. 1999, *The Weight of the World* (trans. P.P. Ferguson), Polity Press: Cambridge.

Bradley, G., 1992, "Increasing Student Retention Rates," *Youth Studies Australia* 11: 37–42.

Bradley, G., and Stock, J., 1993, *Students at Risk: Identification and Intervention, a Case Study,* set, no. 1.

Braithwaite, J., 1989, *Crime, Shame and Reintegration,* Cambridge University Press: Cambridge.

Bridgeman, P., and Davis, G., 2000, *Australian Policy Handbook,* Allen & Unwin: Sydney.

Burchell, G., Gordon, C., and Miller, P. (eds.), 1991, *The Foucault Effect: Studies in Governmentality,* Harvester-Wheatsheaf: London.

Bureau of Industry Economics, 1989, *Globalisation: Implications for Australian Information Technology Industry,* AGPS: Canberra.

Burt, C., 1925, *The Young Delinquent,* University of London Press: London.

Butler, K., 1997, "The Anatomy of Resilience," *Family Therapy Networker,* March–April 22: 31–37.

Campbell, C., 1998, *The Myth of Social Action,* Cambridge University Press: Cambridge.

Carrington, K., 1993, *Offending Girls,* Allen & Unwin: Sydney.

Caspi, A., Henry, B., McGee, R., Moffitt, T., and Silva, P., 1995, "Temperamental Origins of Child and Adolescent Behaviour Problems," *Child Development,* vol. 57: 357–406.

Cass, B., 1988, *Income Support for the Unemployed in Australia: Towards a More Active System,* AGPS: Canberra.

Castells, M., 1996, *The Rise of the Network Society* (vol. 1) *The Information Age, Economy, Society and Culture,* Blackwell: Oxford.

Castells, M., 1998, *End of Millennium. The Information Age: Economy, Society and Culture,* (vol. 3) Blackwell: Oxford.

Castles, F. G., Gerritsen, R., and Vowles, R. (eds.), 1996, *The Great Experiment: Labour Parties and Public Policy Transformation in Australia and New Zealand,* Allen & Unwin: Sydney.

Catalano, R., 1998, Young People in Communities Forum, Hosted by the Victorian Department of Human Service, Melbourne.

Catalano, R., Hawkins, J., Krenz, C., Gillmore, M., Morrison, D., Wells, E., and Abbott, R., 1993, "Using Research to Guide Culturally Appropriate Drug Abuse Prevention," *Journal of Consulting and Clinical Psychology,* vol. 61: 804–11.

Catalano, R. F., and Hawkins, J. D., 1996. "The Social Development Model: A Theory of Antisocial Behaviour," in J. D. Hawkins (ed.), *Delinquency and Crime: Current Theories,* Cambridge University Press: New York, pp. 149–97.

Catley, B., 1996, *Globalising Australian Capitalism,* Cambridge University Press: Melbourne.

Cerny, P. G., 1991, *The Structural Transformation of Politics,* Sage: London.

Chamberlain, C., and MacKenzie, D., 1998, *Youth Homelessness: Early Intervention and Prevention,* Australian Centre for Equity through Education: Sydney.

Chipman, L., 1984, "Jailing Australia"s Children," *Quadrant,* January: 36–43.

Ciccourel, A., 1968, *Social Organization and Juvenile Justice,* Heineman Education: Loundon.

Clarke, H., 1998, "Dumbing Down in Australian Universities," *Quadrant*, September: 55–60.
Cloward, R., and Ohlin, L., 1960, *Delinquency and Opportunity: A Theory of Delinquent Gangs*, The Free Press: New York.
Cohen, S., 1985, *Visions of Crime, Punishment and Classification*, Polity Press: London.
Compass, B., Hinden, J., and Gerhardt, C., 1995, "Adolescent Development: Pathways of Risk and Resilence," *Annual Review of Psychology*, vol. 46: 265–93.
Constable, E., and Burton, K., 1993, "Prevention and Politics: Giving At-risk Youth a Future," in D. Evans, M. Myhill, and J. Izard (eds.), *Students "Behaviour Problem: Positive Initiative and New Frontiers*, ACER: Hawthorn, 16–24.
Cordray, D., and Pion, G., 1997, What"s Behind the Numbers? Definitional Issues in Counting the Homeless, In D. Culhane and S. Hornburg (eds.), *Understanding Homelessness: New Policy and Research Perspectives*, Fannie Mae Foundation: Washington.
Danziger, K., 1990, *Constructing the Subject: Historical Origins of Psychological Research*, Cambridge University Press: Cambridge.
Davis, M., 1992, *City of Quartz*, Verso Books: London.
Davis, P., and Hersh, R., 1987, "Rhetoric and Mathematics", in J. Nelson, A. Megill and D. McCloskey (eds.), *The Rhetoric of the Human Sciences*, University of Wisconsin Press: Madison.
Dean, M., 1994, *Critical and Effective Histories*, Routledge: London.
————. 1999, "Risk, Calculable and Incalculable," in D. Lupton (ed.), *Risk and Sociocultural Theory*, Cambridge University Press: Cambridge.
Dean, M., and Hindess, B. (eds.), 1998, *Governing Australia: Studies in Contemporary Rationalities of Government*, Cambridge University Press: Melbourne.
Debelle, G., and Vickery, J., 1998, "The Macroeconomics of Australian Unemployment," in Economics Group (eds.), *Unemployment and the Australian Labour Market*, Reserve Bank of Australia: Sydney, pp. 235–65.
Department of Employment Education and Training (DEET), 1992 "An Evaluation of the Commonwealth"s Students At Risk Program," DEET: Canberra.
————. 1995, *Youth Bureau Report on Youth Consultations*, DEET: Canberra, cited in Youth Affairs Council of Victoria, submission to Senate Community Affairs Committee Inquiry into the Proposed Social Security Legislation Amendment (Work for the Dole) April 1997.
DEETYA, 1996, *Working Nation: Evaluation of the Employment, Education and Training Elements*, Evaluation and Monitoring Branch, DEETYA: Canberra.
Queensland Department of Family, Youth and Children (QDFYC), 1999, Issues Paper, No. 2: *Causes and Juvenile Delinquency;* GoPrint: Brisbane
Department of Human Service Western Metropolitan Region, 1998, *Service Context and Intervention Approach of the School Focused Youth Services*, Victoria, preliminary discussion paper, no. 1.
Department of Human Services and Health (Commonwealth), 1995, *Youth Suicide In Australia: A Background Monograph*, AGPS: Canberra.
Devine, J., and Wright, J., 1993, *The Greatest Evil: Urban Poverty and the American Underclass*, Aldine Gruyter: New York.

Donzelot, K., 1990, *Constructing the Subject: Historical Origins of Psychological Research*, Cambridge University Press: Cambridge.

Douglas, M., 1974, *Risk and Blame: Essays in Cultural Theory*, Routledge: London.

Dryfoos, J., 1990, *Adolescence at Risk: Prevalence and Prevention*, Oxford University Press: New York.

——. 1994 *Full Service Schools: A Revolution in Health and Social Services for Children, Youth and Families*, San Francisco.

Dugdale, R., 1877, *The Jukes: A Study in Crime, Pauperism and Heredity*, Putnam: New York.

Dwyer, P., 1997a, *Participant Pathways and Outcomes in Vocational Education and Training 1992–1995*, Research Report 14, University of Melbourne: Parkville.

——. 1997b, *Opting Out Early: School Leavers and the Degeneration of Youth Policy*, National Clearing House for Youth Studies: Hobart.

Eckersley, R., 1988, *Casualties of Change: The Predicament of Young People in Australia: A Report on the Social and Psychological Problems Faced by Young People in Australia*, Commission for the Future: Carlton.

——. 1992a, *Youth and the Challenge to Change*, Commission for the Future: Carlton.

——. 1992b, *Apocalypse Now! Youth and the Challenge to Change*, Australia"s Commission for the Future, Essay Series No. 1. ACF: Melbourne.

——. 1993, "The West"s Deepening Cultural Crisis," *The Futurist*, November–December: 8–12.

——. 1995, "Value and Visions: Youth and the Failure of Modern Western Culture," *Youth Studies Australia*, vol. 14, no. 1.

——. 1996a, "Young Australians" View of the Future: Dreams and Expectations," *Youth Studies Australia*, vol. 15, no. 3: 11–17.

——. 1996b, *Having Our Say about the Future: Young People"s Dreams and Expectations for Australia in 2010 and the Role of Science and Technology*, Commonwealth of Australia: Canberra, 60–65.

Edwards, M., 1998, "Rapporteur"s Observations," *Dusseldorp Skills Forum, Australia"s Youth: Reality and Risk*, Dusseldorp Skills Forum, March, Sydney, 22–27.

Edwards, M., with Howard, C., and Miller, R., 2001, *Social Policy, Public Policy: From Problem to Practice*, Allen & Unwin: Sydney.

Elias, N., 1987, "On Human Beings and their Emotions: A Process-Sociological Essay," *Theory, Culture & Society*, vol. 4: 339–61.

Elster, J., 1986, "Introduction," in J. Elster (ed.), *Rational Choice*, Blackwell: Oxford.

Emy, H. V., 1993, *Remaking Australia*, Allen & Unwin: Sydney.

Engel, U., and Strasser, H., 1998, "Note on the Discipline/Notes Sociologiques," *Canadian Journal of Sociology*, vol. 23, no. 1, Winter: 92–103.

EPAC, 1986, *Business Investment and the Capital Stock*, Council Paper No. 10, AGPS: Canberra.

——. 1992, *Unemployment in Australia*, AGPS: Canberra.

——. 1995, *Inequality in Australia*, AGPS: Canberra.

Farrington, D. 1994 "The Influence of the Family on Delinquent Development," in C. Henricson (ed.), *Crime and the Family*, Family Policy Studies Center: London.

———. 1994/1997, "Human Development and Criminal Careers," in M. Maguire, R. Morgan, and R. Reiner (eds.), *The Oxford Handbook of Criminology*, Oxford University Press: Oxford.

———. 1996, *Understanding and Preventing Youth Crime*, Joseph Rowntree Foundation: York.

Fattah, E., 1997, *Criminology, Past, Present and Future: A Critical Overview*, Macmillan: London.

Fergusson, D., and Lynsky, M., 1996, "Adolescent Resiliency to Family Adversity," *Journal of Child Psychology and Psychiatry and Allied Disciplines*, vol. 37, no. 3: 281–92.

Fernandez-Armesto, P., 1998, *Truth: A History and Guide for the Perplexed*, Black Swan: London.

Fincher, R., and Nieuwenhuysen, J. (eds.), 1998, *Poverty Then and Now*, Melbourne University Press: Melbourne.

Finn, B., 1991, *Young People"s Participation in Post-Compulsory Education and Training*, Australian Education Council Review Committee, AGPS: Canberra.

Flyvbjerg, B., 2000, *Practice of the Social Sciences*, Cambridge University Press: Cambridge.

Fonagy, P., Steele, M., Steele, H., and Target, M., 1994, "The Theory and Practice of Resilience," *Journal of Child Psychology, Psychiatry and Allied Disciplines*, vol. 35, no. 2: 213–57.

Foucault, M., 1977, *Discipline and Punish*, Peregrine Books: London.

———. 1980, *Power/Knowledge: Selected Interviews and Other Writings, 1972–1977*, Pantheon: New York.

———. 1991, "Governmentality," in Burchell, G., Gordon, C., and Miller, P. (eds.), *The Foucault Effect: Studies in Governmentality*, Harvester/Wheatsheaf: London.

Frankel, B., 1987, *The Post Industrial Utopians*, Polity: Oxford.

Franklin, J., (ed), 1998, *The Politics of Risk Society*, Polity Press in association with the Institute for Public Policy Research: Cambridge.

Freeland, J., 1996, The Teenage Labour Market and Post-compulsory Curriculum Reform, in *Making It Work: Vocational Educational in Schools Conference*, Melbourne.

Gans, H., 1995, *The War Against the Poor: The Underclass and Anti-poverty Policy*. Basic Books: New York.

Garland, D., 1992, "Criminological Knowledge and Its Relation to Power," *The British Journal of Criminology*, vol. 32, no. 4: 403–22.

———. 1994, "Historical Development and Current Trends," in M. Macquire, R. Morgan and R. Reiner (eds.), *The Oxford Handbook of Criminology*, Clarendon Press: Oxford.

———. 1996, "The Limits of the Sovereign State," *The British Journal of Criminology*, vol. 36, no. 4: 445–71.

———. 2001, *Cultures of Crime Control*, Polity Press: Oxford.

Garmezy, N., 1987, "Resiliency and Vulnerability to Adverse Developmental Outcomes Associated with Poverty," *American Behavioural Scientist*, vol. 34, no. 4: 416–30.

Garmezy, N., and Rutter, M. (eds.), 1983, *Stress, Coping and Development in Childhood*, McGraw-Hill: New York.

Gass, G., 1988, "Towards the Active Society," *OECD Observer*, no. 152: 4–8.

Giddens, A., 1990, *The Consequences of Modernity*, Polity Press: Cambridge.
———. 1995, *Beyond Left and Right*, Polity Press: Cambridge.
Glueck, S., and Glueck, E., 1965, *Physique and Delinquency*, Harper Row: New York.
Gould, S. J., 1996, *Life"s Grandeur*, Jonathan Cape: London.
Gregory, R., 1997a, "Wages Policy and Unemployment in Australia," in *Economica*, vol. 53, supplementary: 53–74.
———. 1997b, "Job Creation: Comparing the United States and Australia," P. James, W. Veit, and S. Wright (eds.), *Work of the Future: Global Perspectives*, Allen & Unwin: Sydney.
Griffin, C., 1993, *Representationms of Youth: The Study of Youth and Adolescence in Britain and America*, Polity Press: Cambridge.
Hacking, I., 1986a, *The Taming of Chance*, Cambridge University Press: Cambridge.
———. 1986b "Making Up People," in T. Heller et al. (eds.), *Reconstructing Individualism*, Stanford University Press: Stanford.
Hagan, J., and McCarthy, B., 1997, *Mean Streets: Youth Crime and Homelessness*, Cambridge University Press: Cambridge.
Haggerty, R., Sherrod, L., Garmezy, N., and Rutter, M. (eds.), 1994. *Stress, Risk and Resilience in Children and Adolescence: Processes, Mechanisms and Interventions*, Cambridge University Press: Cambridge.
Hahn, F., 1973, *On the Notion of Equilibrium in Economics*, Cambridge University Press: Cambridge.
Harris, R., 1993, "Globalisation, Trade and Income," *Canadian Journal of Economics*, vol. 26, no. 2: 753–76.
Hassan, R., and Carr, J., 1989, "Changing Patterns of Suicide in Australia," *Australian and New Zealand Journal of Psychiatry*, 23: 226–34.
Hawkins, J., Arthur, M., and Catalano, R., 1995, "Preventing Substance Abuse," in M. Tonry and D. Farrington (eds.), *Building a Safer Society: Strategic Approaches to Crime Prevention*, vol. 19: 343–427.
Hawkins, J., Herrenkohl, T., Farrington, D., Brewer, D., Catalano, R., and Harachi, T., 1998, "A Review of Predictors of Youth Violence," in R. Loeber and D. P. Farrington (eds.), *Serious and Violent Juvenile Offenders: Risk Factors and Successful Interventions*, Sage: Thousand Oaks, CA 106–46.
Hawkins, J., Lishner, D., Catalano, R., and Howard, M., 1985, "Childhood Predictors of Adolescent Substance Abuse: Towards an Empirically Ground Theory," *Journal of Children in Contemporary Society*, vol. 18: 11–48.
Hawkins, J., and Weis, J., 1985, "The Social Development Model: An Integrated Approach to Delinquency Prevention," *Journal of Primary Prevention*, vol. 2: 73–97.
Hazzell, P., and King, R., 1996, "Arguments for and against Teaching Suicide Prevention in Schools," *Australian New Zealand Journal of Psychiatry*, vol. 30: 633–42.
Health and Community Services, 1995, *Mental Health Services: Current Youth Suicide Prevention Activities in Victoria*, Psychiatric Services Division, HACS: Melbourne.
Henry, S., and Milovanovic, D., 1991, "Constitutive Criminology: The Maturation of Critical Criminology," *Criminology*, vol. 29: 293–315.

―――――. 1994, "The Constitution of Constitutive Criminology: A Postmodern Approach to Criminological Theory," in D. Nelken (ed.), *The Futures of Criminology*, Sage: London.

Herman, A., 1997, *The Idea of Decline in Western History*, The Free Press: New York.

Hewlett, S. A., 1991, *When the Bough Breaks: The Cost of Neglecting Our Children*, Harper Perennial: New York.

Hil, R., 1996, *Making Them Pay: A Critical Review of Parental Restitution in Australia*, Centre for Social and Welfare Research: Townsville.

Hil, R., and McMahon, A., 2001, *Families, Crime and Juvenile Justice*, Peter Lang: New York.

Hogg, R., and Brown, D., 1998, *Rethinking Law and Order*, Pluto: Armadale.

Holloway, W., and Jefferson, T., 1997, "The Risk Society in an Age of Anxiety: Situating Fear of Crime," *British Journal of Sociology*, vol. 48, no. 2: 255–66.

Home Office, 1996, *Tackling the Causes of Crime*, Home Office: London.

Homel, R., Cashmore, J., Gilmore, L., Hayes, A., Lawrence, J., Leech, M., O"Connor I., Vinson, T., Najman J, and Western, J., *Pathways to Prevention: Developmental and Early Intervention Approaches to Crime in Australia, Full Report*, Commonwealth Attorney-General"s Department: Canberra.

Hooton, E., 1939, *The American Criminal*, Harvard University Press: Cambridge.

Hudson, B. 1996, *Understanding Justice*, Open University Press: Buckingham.

Hunt, A., 1999, *Governing Morals: A Social History of Moral Regulation*, Cambridge University Press: Melbourne.

Hunter, I., 1988, *Culture and Government*, Macmillan: London.

Irwin, C. E., and Millstein, S. G., 1986, "Bio-psychological Correlates of Risk-taking Behaviours during Adolescence," *Journal of Adolescent Healthcare*, vol. 7: 82–93.

Jencks, C., and Mayer, S., 1990, "The Social Consequences of Growing Up in a Poor Neighbourhood," In The National Research Council, *Inner City Poverty in the United States*, National Academy Press, Washington, DC, 111–86.

Jones, B., 1982, *Sleepers Wake!* Oxford University Press, Melbourne.

Jones, P., 2001, *Identifying Chronic Juvenile Offenders*, paper presented to British Criminology Conference, July.

Kalafat, J., and Elias, M., 1995, "Suicide Prevention in an Educational Context, in Broad and Narrow Foci", *Suicide and Life Threatening Behaviour*, vol. 25: 123–133.

Kalafat, J., and Galiana, C., 1996, "The Use of Simulations to Assess the Impact of an Adolescent Suicide Response Curriculum," *Suicide and Life Threatening Behaviour*, vol. 26: 359–65.

Katz, J., 1988, *Seductions of Crime*, Basic Books: New York.

Kaufman-Osborn, T., 1991, *Politics/Sense/Experience*, Cornell University Press: Ithaca.

Kelly P., 1998, "Risk and the Regulation of Youth(ful) Identities in an Age of Manufactured Uncertainty," unpublished Ph.D. Thesis, Deakin.

King, A., 1998, "Income Poverty since the 1970s," in R. Fincher and J. Nieuwenhuysen (eds.), *Poverty Then and Now*, Melbourne University Press: Melbourne, 71–102.

Kirk, W., 1993, *Adolescent Suicide; A School-based Approach to Assessment and Intervention*, Illinois Research Press.

Bibliography

Kuhn T. S., 1962, *The Nature of Scientific Revolutions*, University of Chicago Press: Chicago.

Landt, J., Fischer, S., and Scott, P., 1997, *Income Distribution*, National Centre for Social and Economic Modelling, ANU: Canberra.

Langmore, J., and Quiggin, J., 1994, *Work for All, Full Employment in the Nineties*, Melbourne University Press: Melbourne.

Last, J., 1988, *A Dictionary of Epidemiology*, Oxford University Press: New York.

Latham, M., 1998, *Civilising Global Capitalism*, Allen & Unwin: Sydney.

Le, A., and Miller, P., 1999, *A Risk Index Approach to Unemployment: An Application Using the Survey of Employment and Unemployment Patterns*, Occasional Paper (ABS 6293.0.00.001), ABS: Canberra

Lepenies, W., 1988, *Between Literature and Science: The Rise of Sociology*, Cambridge University Press: Cambridge.

Leser, D., 1996, "Pauline Hanson"s Bitter Harvest," *The Age Good Weekend*, November 30.

Lindblom, C., 1959, "The Science of Muddling Through," *Public Administration Review*, vol. 19: 78–98.

Lloyd, P., 1995, "The Nature of Globalisation," in EPAC, *Globalisation: Issues for Australia*, EPAC Commission Paper No. 5. AGPS: Canberra, 11–32.

Lowenthal, D., 1995, *The Past is a Foreign Country*, Cambridge University Press: Melbourne.

Luhmann, N., 1979, *Trust and Power*, Wiley: Chichester.

Lupton. D. (ed.), 1999, *Risk and Sociocultural Theory: New Directions and Perspectives* Cambrigde University Press: Melbourne.

Machanie, D., 1991, "Adolescent at Risk: New Directions," *Journal of Adolescent Health*, vol. 12: 838–43.

Manent, P., 1998, *The City of Man*, (trans. M. Le Pain), Princeton University Press: Princeton.

Manne, R., and James, M., "Senator Ryan and the New Universities," unpublished paper.

Mannheim, H., 1955, *Group Problems in Crime and Punishment*, Routledge and Kegan Paul: London.

Marginson, S., 1997, *Markets in Education*, Allen & Unwin: Sydney.

Marvin, W., Sellin, T., and Figlio, R., 1972, *Delinquency in a Birth Cohort*, University of Chicago Press: Chicago.

May, A., and Wildavsky, A., 1978 (eds), *The Policy Cycle*, Sage: Beverly Hills.

McDonald, R. (ed.), 1997, *Youth, the Underclass and Social Exclusion*, Routledge: London.

Merton, R. K., 1969, *On Theoretical Sociology*, Free Press: New York.

Miller, P. W. and Volker, P. A., 1987, *The Youth Labour Market in Australia: A Survey of Issues and Evidence*, Centre for Economic Policy Research, Discussion Paper No. 171, ANU: Canberra.

Ministry of Western Australia, 1993, *Youth Suicide Prevention: A Resource Package for Student Services Personnel*, Supply West item 15458.

Minson, J., 1993, *The Geneaology of Morals*, Routledge: London.

Muncie, J., 1999, *Youth and Crime: A Critical Introduction*, Sage: London.

National Crime Prevention, 1999, *Pathways to Prevention: Developmental and Early Intervention Approaches to Crime in Australia*, Commonwealth Attorney-General"s Department: Canberra.

National Health Medical Research Council Health Advancement Committee, 1996, *Effective School Health Promotion: Towards Health Promoting Schools*, NHMRC: Sydney.

Neil, C., and Fopp, R., 1992, *Homelessness in Australia: Causes and Consequences*, CSIRO: Victoria: Division Building, Constructions and Engineering.

New Labour, 1997, *No More Excuses*, HMSO: London.

Nordau, M., 1982, 1895/1968, *Degeneration* (translated from the 2nd edition), with introduction by G. Mosse, Reprint, Howard Fertig: New York.

Norton, R., 1994, "Adolescent Suicide: Risk Factors and Countermeasures," *Journal of Health Education*, vol. 25, no. 6: 358–61.

O"Connor, I., 1992, *Youth, Crime and Justice in Queensland*, Criminal Justice Commission: Brisbane.

OECD, 1988, *The Future of Social Protection*, OECD Social Policy Studies, no. 6, Paris.

O"Malley, P., 1992, "Risk, Power and Crime Prevention," *Economy and Society*, vol. 21, no. 3: 252–75.

———. 1996, "Post-Social Criminologies: Some Implications of Current Political Trends for Criminology Theory and Practice," *Current Issues in Criminal Justice*, vol. 8, no. 1: 17–32.

O"Neill, J., 1994, *The Missing Child in Liberal Theory*, University of Toronto Press: Toronto.

Pareto, V., 1927/1972, *A Manual of Political Economy*, Macmillan: London.

Park, R., 1915, "The City: Suggestions for the Investigation of Human Behaviour in the City," *American Journal of Sociology*, vol. 20, no. 5: 577–612.

Patton, G., and Burns, J., 1997, *Scope for Preventative Intervention in Youth Suicide: A Risk Factor Approach*, report prepared for the National Health and Medical Research Council.

Pearson, G., 1983, *Hooligans: A History of Respectable Fears*, Macmillan: London.

Peterson, A., Compas, B., Brooks-Gunn, J., Stemmler, M., Ey, S., and Grant, K., 1993, "Depression in Adolescence," *American Psychologist*, vol. 48, no. 2: 155–68.

Pick, D., 1993, *Faces of Degeneration: A European Disorder 1848–1940*, Cambridge University Press: Cambridge.

Pitts, J., 2001 "The New Correctionalism: Young People, Youth Justice and New Labour" in R. Matthews and J. Pitts, 2001, *Crime, Disorder and Community Safety*, Routledge: London.

———. 2001, *The New Politics of Youth Crime: Discipline or Solidarity*, Palgrave: Basingstoke.

———. 2002, "Korrectional Karaoke: New Labor and the Zombification of Youth Justice," in R. Hil and G. Tait (eds.), *Hard Lessons: Reflections on Crime Control in Late Modernity*, Aldershot: Ashgate.

Pitts, J., and Hope, T., 1988, "The Local Politics of Inclusion: The State and Community Safety," *Social Policy and Administration*, vol. 3, No. 5.

Potas, I., Vining, J., and Wilson, P., (eds.), 1990, *Young People and Crime: Costs and Prevention*, Australian Institute of Criminology: Canberra.

Prychitko, D., 1995, "Methodological Individualism and the Austrian School," in Prychitko, D. (ed.), *Individuals, Institutions, Interpretations*, Avebury: Aldershot.

Queensland Criminal Justice Commission, 1992, *Youth, Crime and Justice in Queensland;* Queensland Criminal Justice Commission: Brisbane.

Quiggin, J., 1996, *Great Expectations,* Allen & Unwin: Sydney.

Rehny, N., and McBride, S., 1997, *Help Wanted: Economic Security for Youth,* Canadian Center for Policy Alternatives: Vancouver.

Resnick, M. D., Harris, L. J., and Blum, R. W., 1993, "The Impact of Caring and Connectedness on Adolescent Health and Well-being," *Journal of Pediatrics and Child Health,* vol. 29, supplement 1: 3–9.

Rhoads, J. K., 1991, *Critical Issues in Social Theory,* Pennsylvania State University Press: Philadelphia.

Robertson, R., 1985, "The Relativisation of Societies: Modern Religion and Globalisation," in T. Robbins, H. Shepherd, and J. McBride (eds.), *Cults, Culture and the Law,* Scholars Press: Chicago.

———. 1992, *Globalisation,* Sage: London.

Rock, P., 1994, "The Social Organisation of British Criminology," in M. Maguire, R. Morgan, and R. Reiner (eds.), *The Oxford Handbook of Criminology,* Oxford University Press, Oxford: 125–48.

Rose, N., 1990, *Governing the Soul: The Shaping of the Private Self,* Routledge: London.

———. 1994a, "Expertise and the Government of Conduct," *Studies in Law, Politics and Society,* vol. 14: 259–367.

———. 1994b, "Expertise and the Government of Conduct", *Studies in Law, Politics and Society,* vol. 14: 259–367.

———. 1996, "The Death of the Social? Re-figuring the Territory of Government," *Economy and Society,* vol. 25, no. 3: 327–56.

Rose, S., Lewontin, R., and Kamin, L., 1987, *Not In Our Genes: Biology, Ideology and Human Nature,* Pelican, Harmond South.

Rutter, M., 1985, "Resilience in the Face of Adversity, Protective Factors and Resistance to Psychiatric Disorder," *British Journal of Psychiatry,* vol. 147: 598–611.

Rutter, M., Giller, H., and Hagill, A., 1998, *Antisocial Behaviour by Young People,* Cambridge University Press: Cambridge.

Ryan, W. S., 1975, *Blaming the Victim,* Vintage Books: New York.

Sassan, S., 1991, *The Global City,* Princeton University Press: Princeton.

Schaffer, D., 1993, "Preventing Suicide in Young People," in *Innovations and Research,* vol. 2, no. 4: 3–4.

Schaffer, D., Garland, A., Vieland, V., Underwood M., and Busner, C., 1991, "The Impact of Curriculum-based Suicide Prevention Programs for Teenagers," *Journal of the American Academy of Child and Adolescent Psychiatry,* vol. 30 no. 4: 588–96.

Schutz, A., 1986, *The Correspondence of Alfred Schutz and Aron Gurwisch,* University of Indiana Press: Bloomington.

Schweinhart, L., Barnes, H., and Weikart, D., 1993, *Significant Benefits: The High/Scope Perry Preschool Study through Age 27,* High/Scope Press: Ypsilanti.

Sen, A., 1992, *Inequality Reconsidered,* Oxford University Press: Oxford.

Sennett, R., 1999, *The Corrosion of Character: The Personal Consequences of Work in the New Capitalism,* Norton: New York.

Sercombe, H., 1997, "Naming Youth: The Construction of the Youth Category," unpublished Ph.D. thesis, Murdoch University: Perth.

Seth-Purdie, R., 2001, "Multiple Risk Exposures and Likelihood of Welfare Receipt," *Family Matters*, 57, 46–53.
Shaw, C., and McKay, D., 1931, *Social Factors in Juvenile Delinquency*. USGPO: Washington.
Shragge, E. (ed.), 1997, *Workfare: Ideology for a New Underclass*, Garamond Press: Toronto.
Sibley, D., 1995, *Geographies of Exclusion: Society and Difference in the West*, Routledge: London.
Sidoti, C., 1998, "Civil Rights and Young People: The Next Frontier," *Just Policy*, no. 13 June: 31–38.
Simons, H., 1938, *Personal Income Taxation*, University of Chicago Press: Chicago.
Slee, R., and Knight, T., 1992, "Introduction" in R. Slee (ed.) *Discipline in Australian Public Education: Changing Policy and Practice*, ACER: Hawthorn, 1–13.
Stilwell, F., 1995, "Reworking Australia," in S. Rees and G. Rodley (eds.), *The Human Cost of Managerialism*, Pluto Press: Sydney.
Sumner, C., 1994, *The Sociology of Deviance: An Obituary*, Open University: Buckingham.
Sutherland, E., and Locke, H., 1936, *Twenty Thousand Homeless Men: A Study of Unemployed Men in the Chicago Shelters*, J.B. Lippincott: Philadelphia.
Sweet, R., 1998, Youth: The Rhetoric and the Reality of the 1990 Dusseldorp Skills Forum, *Australia"s Youth: Reality and Risk*, Dusseldorp Skills Forum, March, Sydney, 5–22.
Tait, G., 1993, "Reassessing Street Kids: a Critique of Subcultural Theory," in R. White (ed.), *Youth Subcultures: Theory, History and the Australian Experience*, National Clearinghouse for Youth Studies: Hobart.
Tanner, L., 1999, *Open Australia*, Pluto Press: Sydney.
Taylor, B., 1994, *The Prevention of Youth Suicide and Self Harm: Promoting Intersectoral Action*, Victorian Health Promotion Foundation: Melbourne.
Taylor, I., Walton, P., and Young, J., 1973, *The New Criminology*, Routledge Kegan Paul: London.
Thomas, W. I., 1923, *The Unadjusted Girl: with Cases and Standpoint Analysis*, Little Brown: Boston.
Thompson, K., 1998, *Moral Panics*, Routledge: London.
Thrasher, F., 1927, *The Gang: A study of 1313 Gangs in Chicago*, University of Chicago Press: Chicago.
Tomlinson, J., 1998, "Income Guarantees and Future Choices," in J. Bessant and S. Cook, *Against the Odds: Young People and Work*, Australian Clearinghouse for Youth Studies: Tasmania.
Tversky, A., 1990, "The Psychology of Risk," in W. Sharpe (ed.), *Quantifying the Market Risk Phenomenon for Investment Decisionmaking*, Institute for Chartered Financial Analysts: Charlottesville.
Utting, D., 1994, "Family Factors and the Rise in Crime," in A. Coote (ed.), *Families, Children and Crime*, Institute of Public Policy Research: London.
Utting, D., Bright, J., and Hendrickson, C., 1993, *Reducing Criminality Among Young People: A Sample of Relevant Programmes in the United Kingdom*, Home Office: London.
———. 1994, *Crime and the Family*, Family Policy Studies Center, Paper No. 16: London.

van Parijs, P., 1993, *The Case for Basic Income*, Verso: London.
van Swaaningen, R., 1997, *Critical Criminology*, Sage: London.
Victorian Department of Human Services, 1998, *Communities That Care Program*, Victorian Government Printer: Melbourne.
Vinson, T., 1999, *Unequal in Life: The Distribution of Social Advantage in Victoria and New South Wales*, The Ignatius Social Policy Centre: Sydney.
Walkerdine, V., and Lucey, H., 1989, *Democracy in the Kitchen: Regulating Mothers and Socialising Daughters*, Virago Press: London.
Waters, M., 1995, *Globalisation*, Routledge: London.
Watson, I., 1993, *The Ideology of the Underclass and the Reality of the Working Poor; Long Term Unemployment and Occupational Restructuring* (pp. 14–16), University of New South Wales, Sydney: National Social Policy Conference.
Watts, R., 1993/4, "An Essay on Governmentality," *Arena Journal;* New Series nos. 2/3: 106–65.
————. 2000, "The Right Thing: Globalisation and the State—a Case Study," in S. McBride and J. Wiseman (eds.), *Globalisation and Its Discontents*, Macmillan: London.
Watts, R., Bessant, J., and Hil, R., (in press), *Understanding Criminology: A Critical Introduction*, Polity Press: Cambridge.
Weatherburn, D., 1993, "On the Quest for General Theory of Crime," *Australian and New Zealand Journal of Criminology*, vol. 26, no. 1: 35–46.
West, D., 1982, *Delinquency: Its Roots, Causes and Prospects*, Harvard University Press: Cambridge.
White, R., 1989, "Making Ends Meet: Young People, Work and the Criminal Economy," *Australian New Zealand Journal of Criminology*, vol. 22: 13–24.
————. 1994a, "The Making of a Youth Underclass," *Youth Studies Australia*, vol. 13, no. 1: 18–29.
————. 1994b, "Class, Capitalism and Criminality," Australian New Zealand Society of Criminology, *10th Annual Conference*, September.
————. 1995, "The Poverty of the Welfare State: Managing the Underclass," in H. V. Emy and P. James (eds.), *The State in Question*, Macmillan: Melbourne.
White, R., Aumair, M., Harris, A., McConnell, L., 1997, *Any Which Way You Can: Youth Livelihoods, Community, Resources and Crime*, The Australian Youth Foundation: Sydney.
Whyte, W., 1943, *Street Corner Society*, University of Chicago Press: Chicago.
Wikstrom, D., and Loeder, I., 1997 "Individual Risk Factors, Neighborhood SES and Juvenile Offending," in M. Tonry (ed.), *The Handbook of Crime and Punishment*, Oxford University Press: New York.
Wildavsky, A., and Dake, K., 1990, "Theories of Risk Perception: Who Fears What and Why?" *Daedalus*, no. 116: 41–60.
Williams, J., Ayers, C., and Arthur, M., 1997, "Risk and Protective Factors in the Development of Delinquency and Conduct Disorders," in M. W. Fraser (ed.), *Risk and Resilience in Childhood: An Ecological Perspective*, NASW Press: Washington.
Wilson, B., and Wyn, J., 1987, *Shaping Futures*, Allen & Unwin: Sydney.
Wilson, W., 1996, *When Work Disappears: The World of the New Urban Poor*, Alfred Knopf: New York.

Winefield, A., Tiggemann, M., Winefield, H., and Goldney, R., 1993, *Growing Up with Unemployment: A Longitudinal Study of Its Psychological Impact*, Routledge: London.
Withers, G., and Batten, M., 1995, *Programs for At-Risk Youth: A Review of the American Canadian and British Literature since 1984*, Research Monograph No. 47, Dusseldorp Skills Forum: Sydney.
Wolin, S., and Wolin, S., 1995, "Resilience among Youth: Growing Up in Substance Abusing Families," *Paediatric Clinics of North America*, vol. 42: 415–29.
Wooden, M., 1998, "The Labour Market for Young Australians," Dusseldorp Skills Forum, *Australia"s Youth: Reality and Risk*, Dusseldorp Skills Forum, March, Sydney, 29–50.
Wright, E. O., 1985, *Classes*, Verso: London.
Wuest, J., 1992, "Building a System of Effective Programs for In-school At Risk Youth and Dropout Youth," in Council of Chief State Officers, *Investing in Youth: A Compilation of Recommended Policies*, Conference Report, Washington.
Wundersitz, J., 1993, "Some Statistics on Youth Offending: An Inter-jurisdictional Comparison," in F. Gale, N. Naffine and J. Wundersitz (eds.), *Juvenile Justice; Debating the Issues*, Sydney Allen & Unwin: Sydney.
Wyn, J., and White, R., 1997, *Rethinking Youth*, Allen & Unwin: Sydney.
Yeatman, A., 1990, *Bureaucrats, Femocrats and Democrats: Essays on the Contemporary Australian State*, Allen & Unwin: Sydney.
———. 1998, "Interpreting Contemporary Contractualism," in M. Dean and B. Hindess (eds.), *Governing Australia*, Cambridge University Press: Melbourne.
Young, J., 1999, *The Exclusive Society*, Sage: London.
Youth Justice Board, 2001, *Policy*, http://www.youth-justice-board.gov.uk/policy/policy.htm.

Index

Abbott, 25
Aboriginals, 62
active society, 25
adolescence
    as agonistic, 85–89
    idea of, 29
    and risk, 71–85
adult role, 29
Ainley, C., 32
anti-social youth, 95–102, 108
Arblaster, A., 29, 48, 119
Aries, P., 88
Audit Commission (UK) 101–107
Australian Education Council, 31

basic income, 51
Batten, M., 13, 31, 32, 33, 119
Bauman, Z., 13
Beck, U., 3, 8–11, 16, 50, 120–24, 49, 127
Bell, S., 23, 31
Benjamin, J., 113
Bernstein, P., 8
Bessant, J., 12, 13, 25, 30, 31, 53, 75, 100, 113, 120, 131
Blair, T., 99–102
Boreham, P., 25
Borowski, T., 68
Bourdieu, P., 63
Bradley, D., 32
Braithwaite, J., 82
British crime control policies, 97–114
Brown, D., 71, 110
Burdekin, B., 55
Burton, J., 32

Cambridge Institute of Criminology, 102
Carlyle, T., 68
Carrington, K., 75, 80, 115
Caspi, A., 91
Cass, B., 26
Castells, M., 25

Catley, R., 1, 33
causes; causality, 126
    and crime, 100–111
    and unemployment, 41–48
central tendency, measures of, 61
Cerny, P., 23
Chamberlain, C., 5, 53–63
Chicago school, 76
childhood, 87–88
Cicourel, A., 66
Clarke, H., 34
class and homelessness, 63
Cohen, S., 84–87
Commonwealth of Australia, National Crime Prevention, 73, 75–77
Common Youth Allowance, 29, 118–120
Comte, A., 8
Constable, E., 31–2
contractualism, 23
crime, 4, 25–26, 71–95
    control and prevention policies, 97–114, 115–119
    conventional understanding of, 72–3
    general theory of, 78–80
    and risk 74–77
    and urban poor 74–79
Cordray, D., 53
crime problem, 71
crime rate as social facts, 68
Criminal Justice Commission, 68–85
criminology, 20, 67
    as governmentality, 20
critique of causal determinism, 90–91
critique of deviancy theory, 90–91

"dangerous classes," 115–117
Danziger, K., 55, 58, 124
Davis, W., 44, 46, 114
Dean, M., 3, 16–21, 39, 54
Debelle, G., 37

Index

Deet, M., 31
deficit theory, 33–38
delinquency, 31, 71
   and risk, 74–76, 84–86, 87–92
Department of Employment
   Education and Training (DEET),
   38, 39
deprivation theories, 109–111
developmental psychology and
   risk, 75–77, 78–82
deviance theory, 2, 15
   critique of, 90–93
dole bludger, 39
Douglas, M., 13
Dow, G., 25
drug use, 31
Dryfoos, J., 31–32, 118
Durkheim, E., 55–56

early intervention, 103–5
Eckersley, R., 30, 118
Economic Policy Advisory Council
   (EPAC), 37
education
   and risk, 115–120
   and unemployment, 116
Edwards, M., 32, 119
Elias, N., 72
Elster, J., 24
empirical measures of risk, 32, 51
empirical research, 72
Enlightenment, 11
epidemiological research, 62
experts, 13

family and risk, 88–93, 100–102,
   108–110, 116
Farrington, D., 83, 100, 102–105, 127
fear of lower orders, 115
Fincher, R., 2
Flyvbjerg, B., 72
Fopp, R., 53
Foucault, M., 3, 50, 70
   on government, 16–18, 124
Frankel, B., 51
Franklin, J., 120
Freeland, J., 32
full employment, 124

gangs, 95
Garland, D., 21, 25, 70, 75–77, 97
Gass, R., 25
Giddens, A., 9, 23, 31, 56,
Gill, A., 112
globalisation, 1, 15
Gould, S., 61
government
   concept of, 4–5,
   and risk, 16–27
   of problem populations, 113–126
   processes of, 19–21
   social science and, 114
Gregory, B., 34, 36
Griffin, C., 87, 117
Habermas, J., 11
Hagan, J., 5, 53, 62–68, 123–25
Hagill, R., 118
Hahn, F., 38
Hall, G. Stanley, 88
Herman, J., 14
Hersh, J., 44, 46
Hil, R., 25, 97
Hindess, B., 3, 17–22, 54
Hogg, R., 71, 110
Holloway, T., 12
homelessness, 3, 31, 53–67
hooligans, 14
Hopes, J., 114
Howard, J., 29
Hudson, B., 75
Hunt, A., 113
Hunter, I., 19

incomplete education, 32
individualism, 10, 22–24, 47–48,
   108–113
institutional sites of government,
   19–20
intelligence quotient, 85

James, M., 34
Jefferson, T., 12
Jones, B., 33
Jones, R., 114
juvenile justice in Britain, 97–114
Kamin, L., 87,
Katz, J., 72, 90
Kelly, P., 8, 12, 13, 31, 86–87, 85, 130

Kennedy, J., 83, 84
Kinsey, A., 80
Knight, T., 19
labour markets
    and schooling, 32,
    idea of, 38–43
Langmore, J., 31
Lash, S., 9
Latham, M., 1, 15
Le, A., 39–48
Lepenies, W., 68
Lewontin, R., 88
liberalism, 15
    and risk, 15, 22–26
lifecycle, 84–85, 103–107, 118
Lindblom, C., 4
Loeder, C., 114
Lombroso, C., 22
longitudinal studies, 82–83, 102–106,
loss of confidence, 11
Lowenthal, R., 120
Lupton, M., 8, 99, 100

MacKenzie, D., 5, 53, 54–63
maladjustment and risk, 83–91
Manent, 53, 72
Manne, A., 34
Marginson, S., 13, 32
markets, 24
    idea of, 36
May, J., 4
McCarthy, B., 5, 53, 59–68, 121–22
McCurry, D., 31
metaphors, 23–24
Miller, P., 39–48
Mills, C. Wright, 49
Minson, J., 18
modernity, 9
moral panics, 115–16
Muncie, C., 97, 98, 99, 101
mutual responsibility, 22–23

National Crime Prevention project, 72–75, 85–87, 118–19
Neil, J., 53
neoclassical criminology, 75
neoclassical economics, 15, 122

explaining unemployment, 34–38
neoliberalism, 22–26
New Labour and crime, 97–102
Nieuwenhuysen, P., 2
non-English-speaking background people, 62
nostalgia and risk, 119–20

objectivity in social science, 55, 127
O"Connor, I., 73–75, 83
OECD, 25,
O"Neill, J., 125
Operationalisation, 58–59

Pareto, V., 38
Pathways report, 80–91
Pearson, G., 14, 114, 116
persistent offenders, 102
Pick, D., 15
Pion, N., 53
Pitts, J., 97–100, 105, 108, 111–13
populations at risk, 69–70, 73–74, 118–121
postmodernity, 9
Potas, I., 74
problematisation, 20, 74–84
problem populations, 74–80
Prychitko, V., 37–38

Queensland Criminal Justice Commission, 73–75
Queensland Department of Family, Youth and Children, 73, 78–82
Quiggin, J., 31

rational economic man, 37
reasoning, 22
reductionism, 111–113
research methodology 55–58
restructuring 1, 30
risk, 1,
    concept of, 7
    Beck"s definition, 9–10
    and crime 67–92
    defined, 8, 9–13
    discourse, 2, 21
    early intervention 101–2
    factors, 12, 73–78, 89–90, 100–107

family, 84–86, 101–103
government, 16–26
and individualism, 117–19
and lifecycle, 86–88, 103–108, 115, 124
and neoliberal policies, 21–24, 113
and nostalgia, 119–22
indicators, 2, 73–78, 90, 92, 100–107
management, 2, 112
norms of, 114
and schools, 115–16
risk society, 8–11
Rorty, R., 68
Rose, N., 3, 17, 25, 85, 114, 124, 129
Russell, C., 12, 33, 116
Rutter, M., 116
Ryan, W. S., 36, 39, 66, 67

scales of risk, 81–84
schools, 117–24
Schweinhart, W., 93
Schutz, A., 75
science of risk, 53
Scott, A., 15
Sen, A., 15
Sennett, R., 11
Seth-Purdie, J., 40
settlement houses, 108
Sibling Study, 78–80, 82–87, 125–27
Sidoti, C., 70
Simons, W., 36
Slee, R., 19
"Sleeping Beauty" model of science, 55–56
social control theory, 16
social facts, 56–57
    crime as, 68–71
social pathology, 5
social problems, 2, 12, 25–26, 114
social sciences, 3
    conventional, 4–5
    as nihilism, 74
    and risk 24–26
Stock, W., 32
street crime, 73
subjects of risk research, 76–79
Sumner, C., 92

Sweet, R., 121

Tait, G., 13, 127
Tarde, G., 22
Taylor, I., 76
Thatcher, M., 24
Third Way politics, 15
Thomas, C., 31
Thomas, W. I., 14
Thompson, E. P., 65
Tomlinson, J., 51
Tversky, A., 11

underclass,
    concept of, 2
    urban populations, 74–79, 103–107, 115
unemployment, 3, 24, 29–50
    explaining 33–38
    deficits of unemployed, 33
    deficient schooling and, 33–34
    risk factors, 39–48
    critique of risk factor approach, 41–48, 111–24
Utting, M., 101, 110, 125

van Parijs, P., 51
van Swaaningen, A., 11
Vickery, C., 37
victim-blaming discourses, 39
Vining, I., 73
Vinson, T., 116
Volker, D., 39

Wallace, I., 25
Walton, P., 76
Watts, R., 1, 18, 51, 113
Webber, R., 94
welfarism and crime, 99
West, D. J., 81, 110, 126
White, R., 30, 80, 116, 118
Wikstrom, J., 114
Wildavsky, A., 4
Wilson, B., 50
Wilson, P., 73
Withers, G., 31
Wooden, M., 31, 116
Work
    and adult role, 30

and identity, 48
Wright, E. O., 66
Wynn, J., 50

Yeatman, A., 23
Young, J., 76, 98, 114
youth at risk, 17–18, 29–30, 52–60,
    94–99, 106–114, 115–119, 121–26
youth crime , 97–114
youth homelessness, 53–60
Youth Inclusion Programs, 108
Youth Justice Board (UK) 107–109
youth suicide, 31, 118
youth unemployment, 10, 29–31,
    115–26

 # ERUPTIONS
New Thinking across the Disciplines

Erica McWilliam
General Editor

This is a series of red-hot women's writing after the "isms." It focuses on new cultural assemblages that are emerging from the de-formation, breakout, ebullience, and discomfort of postmodern feminism. The series brings together a post-foundational generation of women's writing that, while still respectful of the idea of situated knowledge, does not rely on neat disciplinary distinctions and stable political coalitions. This writing transcends some of the more awkward textual performances of a first generation of "feminism-meets-postmodernism" scholarship. It has come to terms with its own body of knowledge as shifty, inflammatory, and ungovernable.

The aim of the series is to make this cutting edge thinking more readily available to undergraduate and postgraduate students, researchers and new academics, and professional bodies and practitioners. Thus, we seek contributions from writers whose unruly scholastic projects are expressed in texts that are accessible and seductive to a wider academic readership.

Proposals and/or manuscripts are invited from the domains of: "post" humanities, human movement studies, sexualities, media studies, literary criticism, information technologies, history of ideas, performing arts, gay and lesbian studies, cultural studies, post-colonial studies, pedagogics, social psychology, and the philosophy of science. We are particularly interested in publishing research and scholarship with international appeal from Australia, New Zealand, and the United Kingdom.

For further information about the series and for the submission of manuscripts, please contact:

>Erica McWilliam
>Faculty of Education
>Queensland University of Technology
>Victoria Park Rd., Kelvin Grove Q 4059
>Australia

To order other books in this series, please contact our Customer Service Department at:

>(800) 770-LANG (within the U.S.)
>(212) 647-7706 (outside the U.S.)
>(212) 647-7707 FAX

Or browse online by series at:
>www.peterlangusa.com